Pitman Examinations
English for Speakers of Other Languages

Practice Tests – All levels

Teacher's Guide

The longman dictionary of contemporary English

Felicity O'Dell

Longman

Longman Group UK Limited,
Longman House, Burnt Mill, Harlow,
Essex CM20 2JE, England
and Associated Companies throughout
the world.

First published 1992

ISBN 0 582 076684

Set in 10/12pt Times
Printed in the United Kingdom by Scotprint,
Musselburgh

Acknowledgements

I should like to thank Lois Warden of the
Pitman Examinations Institute for
answering so many questions and for
her many helpful comments on the
manuscript, Susan Davies for her
invaluable help throughout the production
of this series, Richard West for checking
Table One and colleagues and students at
Eurocentre, Cambridge, whose
experiences with the Pitman Exams have
helped a great deal in the production of
both the Teacher's Guide and the five
practice test books.

I should also like to thank Lila Avramidou,
Matoula Dimitrakaki, Dora Fimi,
Barbara Schullian, Athina Kotsi, Maria Papassideri,
Sandra Klapsi, Georgia Sovolaki, Rena Tsiakoumi,
Ritsa Theodoraki, Takis Tsakiris, Ionna Malliou and
the Omiros School, Athens, Greece, for their help in the
preparation of this series.

We are indebted to Longman Group UK Ltd on behalf
of the English Speaking Union for permission to
reproduce Table 1 adapted from 'General & Social
English' Table from *ESU Framework* by
Brendan J. Carroll & Richard West pp18–19.
© English Speaking Union, 1989.

Contents

Introduction

This book contains all the information you need to help candidates prepare for one or more of the five Pitman ESOL examinations. It accompanies the five *Pitman ESOL Practice Tests* published by Longman for the Pitman ESOL examinations. It contains

a) general information about the examinations
b) listening scripts for each of the five levels
c) teaching notes for each of the five levels
d) an answer key for each of the tests in the five *Pitman ESOL Practice Tests*.

Before preparing candidates for any of the exams, teachers are strongly recommended to read the introductory notes which follow. These answer the questions which candidates – and their teachers – most frequently ask about the examinations.

Further information about the examinations can be obtained from the address below:

Pitman Examinations Institute
Godalming
Surrey
GU7 1UU
Tel: 0483 415311

What is the aim of the Pitman examinations?

The overall aim of the exams is to provide a set of exams at a wide range of levels to test candidates' ability to carry out particular language tasks within a context. The exams have been based on the kind of work done in the modern language classroom as well as on the sort of tasks that students may meet in real-life situations. They, therefore, differ from some exams in that they do not focus on grammatical accuracy at the expense of authenticity.

How widely recognised are the examinations?

Pitman examinations are taken in over seventy countries throughout the world and Pitman is the second largest British examinations board conducting examinations in English as a Foreign Language. A pass at Higher Intermediate or Advanced level is recognised as evidence of an appropriate level of English for entry to a number of institutions of higher education in the UK, Australia and other countries. Candidates wishing to know what entry requirements any particular university or college requires would need to write directly to the institution concerned.

What is the right level of exam for my students?

The exam has five levels. The names of the exams at each level suggest fairly clearly what the level of each particular exam is. Pitman's assessment of what is expected at each of the levels is given below and on the next page:

Basic: The candidate can operate in English only to communicate basic needs in short, often inaccurately and inappropriately worded messages. The candidates can understand such simple things as labels, simple signs, street names, prices, etc. but really does not have sufficient language to cope with normal day-to-day real-life communication.

Elementary: The candidate has a basic command of the language which is sufficient for simple practical needs. In more exacting situations, errors and inaccuracies in both production and comprehension cause problems and normal communication breaks down or is difficult to keep going.

Intermediate: The candidate uses the language independently and effectively, coping with overall meaning in unfamiliar situations. Rather frequent lapses in accuracy, fluency, style or comprehension cause some misunderstanding and communication blocks. The candidate usually succeeds in communicating or understanding the general message.

Higher Intermediate: The candidate has a generally effective command of the language but with noticeable lapses in accuracy, appropriacy or comprehension, and some lack of fluency. In spite of these lapses, communication is effective on most occasions and is easily restored when difficulties arise.

Advanced: The candidate uses the language fully, effectively and confidently in most situations. There are a few lapses in accuracy, appropriacy or comprehension but communication is effective and consistent.

The information in the box above comes from the very helpful booklet, *Examinations in English for Speakers of Other Languages: A Guide for Teachers* written by Susan Davies and available from the Pitman Examinations Institute at the address given on page 4.

The vocabulary and structures used in the Pitman exams are also explicitly linked to the levels of the Longman Structural Readers. Most of the input (apart from that in Listening Part 3 and Reading Part 3) corresponds to the Longman guidelines as set out below:

Basic – Pre-Stage One
Elementary – Stage One
Intermediate – Stage Two
Higher Intermediate – Stage Three
Advanced – Stage Four.

However, in the interests of variety and authenticity, words and expressions used may fall outside the Longman lists occasionally.

The most systematic indication of the level of each exam is provided in the *ESU Framework*, a study by Brendan Carroll and Richard West (Longman, 1989).

This study compares the levels of all the different British EFL examinations in a thorough and objective way.

Table One on page 6 is based on the *ESU Framework* and it shows the relationship between the Pitman examinations and other well-known tests. For precise information about what each level actually means, refer to Carroll and West or to the *ESU Framework Chart*. This is a convenient poster summarising the information in the book and it is available from the English Speaking Union, Dartmouth House, 37 Charles Street, London W1X 8AB.

ESU level	Pitman	IELTS	UCLES	UCLES RSA (CCSE)	Oxford	ARELS	Trinity	LCCI SEFIC
9		9						
8		8			Diploma		12	
7	Advanced	7	CPE	4			11	Advanced
6	Higher Int.	6	CAE	3	Higher	Higher	10	Int.
5	Int.	5	FCE	2			9 8	Threshold
4		4					7 6	
3	Elem.	3	PET	1	Prelim	Prelim	5 4	Prelim.
2	Basic	2					3 2 1	
1		1						

Table One: Comparative levels of major EFL examinations

What is the format of the exams?

At each level the exam follows the same format. Table Two summarises that format. Each of the *Pitman ESOL Practice Tests* has a version of this table appropriate to the specific level.

SECTION	DESCRIPTION	% OF MARKS
Section A Listening	**Part One** There are ten questions here. Candidates have to choose which of four answers in their answer book is a good response to what they hear.	30%
	Part Two Candidates have to listen to instructions and do what they are asked to do. They might, for example, have to label a diagram or draw a picture.	
	Part Three Candidates have to listen to something and select what is important for the task. At the higher three levels candidates only hear this part of the listening test once.	
Section B Reading and Writing	**English Usage** Candidates have a text with blanks in it and they have to find one word to fit each blank. At the three lower levels, candidates are given a list of words to choose from when filling the blanks.	15%
	Reading Part One Candidates have five short texts. In each a phrase or sentence is missing. They are given a set of four options and have to decide which option fits best.	30%
	Reading Part Two Candidates read a text and then have to do something to show they understand the text. They may, for example, have to complete a chart.	
	Reading Part Three Candidates have to read a longer text and then, perhaps, fill in a form or label a diagram.	
	Reading and Writing Candidates read something and then have to write something based on what they have read.	10%
	Writing Candidates have to write a composition. They can choose from four different subjects.	15%

Table Two: The format of the Pitman ESOL examinations

At each level the listening section takes about 20 minutes.
The Reading and Writing section differs from level to level:
    Basic and Elementary: 1 hour 40 minutes.
    Intermediate: 2 hours 10 minutes
    Higher Intermediate and Advanced: 2 hours 40 minutes

What is the testing purpose of the various questions?

The aim of each of the questions in the exam is summarised below.

Listening One: to test understanding of interactional English that is likely to be spoken rather than written.
Listening Two: to test the ability to complete a task by following instructions in English. Every detail of what the candidate hears will be important here.
Listening Three: to test the ability to sift what is relevant from what is not relevant from a piece of spoken English and to convert that relevant information into an appropriate written form.
English Usage: to test the ability to choose the correct word to fit in a gap. The words tested are, usually, structural words.
Reading One: to test the ability to understand how information is structured within a text.
Reading Two: to test total understanding of a text by requiring students to follow instructions and convert the information into an appropriate written form. This exercise parallels Listening Two.
Reading Three: to test the ability to scan a text and select the relevant information needed in order to perform a given task. This exercise parallels Listening Three.
Reading and Writing: to test the ability to follow detailed instructions and to write a piece which accordingly follows a given format, uses an appropriate style and covers the content specified.
Writing: to assess the ability to produce a free piece of writing.

What is special about the exams?

There are a number of points that are perhaps worth highlighting as being special about these exams. Some of them will, of course, be more significant to you and your students than others.

1 They are available in a range of five levels.
2 They are concerned more with communicative competence than total accuracy.
3 They do not require the candidate to demonstrate their speaking ability.

4 Candidates may use English-English dictionaries if they wish.
5 In the listening section candidates listen to teachers reading the script ; they do not listen to a cassette (unless, of course, centres choose to make their own cassette from the script sent by PEI).
6 The exams are relatively cheap.
7 They are available on demand as is convenient for centres.
8 The certificate a successful candidate receives looks good. On the back of the certificate there is an outline of what Pitman examinations consist of and a description of what each of the five levels signifies.

How many marks are required to pass the exam?

A candidate needs to obtain 60% of the possible marks in order to pass a Pitman ESOL examination. The papers of all candidates who get 57% to 59% are automatically reassessed by the examiner.
Candidates at Intermediate, Higher Intermediate and Advanced levels will be awarded a First Class pass if they achieve a score of 75% or more – provided that their marks do not fall below approximately 75% in either the Reading and Writing question or the Writing question. As far as the other questions are concerned, a higher mark in Reading, say, will compensate for a lower one in Listening.
Candidates who fail the examination will be given an indication of what their weaknesses were and why they failed.

Is it necessary to pass all sections of the exam?

It is not necessary to pass all sections of the exam. The only regulation which looks at the marks for individual questions is the one governing the awarding of first class passes as described in the previous paragraph.

How is the exam marked?

The system of marking used by PEI ESOL exams is a positive one in that marks are awarded for what is done well rather than deducted for what is done badly. More details about the marking schemes are provided below.

Listening One: One mark for each answer.
Listening Two and Three: There are ten marks for each of these questions. Usually one mark is awarded for each point which a student has to write or respond to. Occasionally two marks may be awarded for one particularly difficult part of a question.
English Usage: Fifteen marks are given for this question at all levels and so there is only a simple one gap one mark relationship at elementary level. At Basic level marks are scaled up and at the higher levels they are scaled down.
Reading One: Two marks for each correct answer.
Reading Two and Three: As with Listening Two and Three, there are ten marks for each of these questions. Usually one mark is awarded for each point which a student has to write or respond to. Occasionally two marks may be awarded for one particularly difficult part of a question.
Reading and Writing: A maximum of five marks is awarded for each of these aspects of a candidate's work – mechanics, range, purpose achieved and impression. The kinds of things which examiners will be looking for under each of these headings are:

> **Mechanics**: grammatical accuracy, spelling, punctuation and handwriting (where this would be a barrier to understanding).
> **Range**: of structures, lexis, cohesive devices, sentence length, clause types and so on.
> **Purpose achieved**: i.e. has the student read the question and done exactly what he or she was asked to do? It is also important here that an appropriate style and register have been chosen.
> **Impression**: this allows examiners to give an overall impression mark for relevance of tone, fluency and appropriacy. It sometimes serves to help candidates whose work is original and seems to have a special flair but perhaps lacks accuracy.

The marks awarded in the way described are then divided by two to provide a final mark of up to ten for this question.

Writing: A maximum of five marks is awarded for each of these aspects of a candidate's work as described more fully above – mechanics, range and impression.

In either of the Writing questions candidates who write too much will not have the excess part of their work assessed. Candidates who write too little will have their potential maximum mark reduced proportionately. It is, thus, important to write to the length stated.

How best can I prepare my students for these examinations?

The first most important thing to do is to make sure that your candidates enter the exam at the appropriate level. The information provided on pages 6 to 7 should help you to do this. If your students are still uncertain about which level to enter for and they do not have time to try a complete exam at the levels they are considering, suggest that they perhaps base their decision on how they feel about the English Usage question at the different levels.
The exams have been based on current teaching practice exemplified in modern coursebooks and so candidates do not need masses of specific teaching of exam techniques. It is, of course, essential that candidates work through all the practice tests available at their level. They will, then, know what to expect from the exam and how to deal with it.
At the beginning of each of the *Pitman ESOL Practice Tests* there is a section called Exam Help. This deals with important aspects of the language tested by the exams. It focuses on the areas that candidates find most difficult in the exams and it gives advice on how to approach each of the sections in turn. Working through the Exam Help section will help your students to get much better marks in the exam.
Finally, it is probably worth pointing out to your students that the Listening part of the exam often seems much more difficult for many candidates under exam conditions than it does in an ordinary class situation. Encouraging your students not to panic if this does seem to be the case but to keep calm and do as well as they possibly can should help them to keep their head on the day. Further information about common problems which students have can be obtained by

writing for the Examinations Report which is published annually by the Pitman Examinations Institute (available from the address given on page 4). The points raised by these reports have, however, been dealt with in the Exam Help sections of the *Pitman ESOL Practice Tests*.

How can using a dictionary help my students in the exams?

A feature of the Pitman examinations is that candidates may use English-English dictionaries during the exam. Different teachers like to give different advice about this. Some prefer their students not to use dictionaries at all as it is certainly very easy to waste a lot of time looking up every unfamiliar word in, say, the Reading Three question where difficult lexis is deliberately included but not tested.

However, sensible dictionary use can help the student in two main ways. Firstly, examiners' reports regularly complain that candidates' main problem is not reading the rubric carefully. If candidates do not understand something in the rubric properly they should certainly look it up in their dictionary. Everything in a rubric is important. The second way in which a dictionary can help is most important at the higher levels. When candidates are in doubt over gaps in the English Usage section a good dictionary can often help. One thing often tested in this question, for instance, is prepositions. A good dictionary for learners of English, such as the *Longman Dictionary of Contemporary English*, for example, will provide information about which prepositions are associated with particular words.

Pitman ESOL Practice Tests – Basic Level

Exam Help

Listening

p.7 ex. 1
Personal details for dictation.

James Quentin   30
19 Hobart Road, London
081 254 2895

Sally Fox   24
48 Smithy Lane, Oxted
0298 337 6549

Rowena Blackie   18
21B Wigmore Street, Peterborough
0674 33485

p.7 ex. 2
Answers
The shapes are, from left to right, a circle, a square, a rectangle or an oblong and a triangle.

p.8 ex. 4
Answers

What's the time?	Half past six.
How old are you?	Fifteen.
Can you swim?	Yes, I can.
How much is it?	Ten dollars.
Are you a teacher?	No, I'm not.
How are you?	Fine, thanks.
Where do you come from?	Mexico City.
Would you like some coffee?	Yes, please.
Is this your book?	No, it isn't.

p. 8 ex. 6
Answers

I'm tired.	Me too.
She lives in London.	Does she?
I'll see you tomorrow.	OK. Goodbye!
It's a lovely day, isn't it!	Isn't it beautiful!
I'd like an ice cream.	Me too.

p.9 ex. 7
Text to read to the students.
You are at the Railway Station. Come out of the station on to Station Street. Walk along Station Street and take the third turning on the left. That's New Road. The building you want is just past the cinema, on the right-hand side of the road. Where are you? (The bus station.)

p. 9 ex. 9
Text to read to the students.
a   When you're in the town could you please buy me some things? Could you please get me a kilo of pota-toes. You are going by car, aren't you? I also need a loaf of white bread. And while you're at the baker's you could buy me a packet of chocolate biscuits too. I love them. Could you also get me a magazine, the one called *She*. I hope they'll still have some in the shop. And the last thing is a bottle of lemonade. It's really kind of you. I'll do the same for you next time I go into town. OK?

b   I met someone yesterday who really wants to meet you and I said you would perhaps telephone her some time soon. Her name is Amanda Jones, that's A-M-A-N-D-A, J-O-N-E-S. She works in the new library in town. She lives near to the library too, in flat 7, 28, Irvine Road, that's I-R-V-I-N-E, Road, that's in Newtown, of course. She says she's in most evenings if you want to ring her and her number is 339764.

c   They're flying to Australia tomorrow and would be really grateful if you could possibly take them to the airport. Their flight is QA 512 - it's with Qantas, the Australian airline – and it leaves at 11.30. So it would be a good idea to leave home at nine or soon after. It's a terribly long flight, of course. It takes just over a day. They should arrive in Melbourne at 1 p.m. tomorrow - our time.

Answers
a) 1 kilo of potatoes, loaf of white bread, packet of chocolate biscuits, *She* magazine, bottle of lemonade
b) Amanda Jones, Flat 7, 28 Irvine Road, Newtown, 339764
c) QA 512, 11.30, 1 p.m. (the next day)

English Usage

p.10
Answers

1	has	6	They
2	with	7	is
3	do	8	on
4	for	9	are
5	It	10	and

p.11
Answers

1	am	6	at
2	my	7	to
3	with	8	it
4	for	9	or
5	have	10	do

Reading One

pp.12-13 ex. 1
Answers
B; D; C; A; D.

pp.13-14 ex. 2
Answers
a they work in the same school
b on a lot of different islands
c Saturday 6th June
d India, Japan and Peru
e It is very old
f I am on holiday then
g Most of the population lives

Reading Two

p.15 ex. 1
Answers
The cat is under the bed; The fish is in the bowl; The dog is next to the fish bowl; The mouse is between the bowl and the bed; The cow is behind the bed; The sheep is on the table; The little girl is in front of the table; The horse is near to the little girl; The bird is above the sheep.

p.16 ex. 2
Answers
The man is wearing glasses, a jacket, trousers, shoes, a shirt and socks.
The woman is wearing a hat, a sweater, a skirt and boots and she is carrying gloves in one hand and a handbag in the other.

p. 16 ex. 3
Answers
The actions in the left-hand column are climbing, sitting, falling and sleeping.
The actions in the right-hand column are driving, running, walking, riding and standing.

Reading Three

pp.17-18
Answers
1 Mongolia; Nearly 2,000,000; Ulan Bator. 2 Alfred Bernhard; Swedish; 1969. 3 Regent; 48; 0245 345765. 4 4; soldier; Lucrezia. 5 1928; 1,000,000; 2,000.

Reading and Writing

pp.19-20 ex. 1
Answers
Dear Sam,

I am having a great holiday in Sweden. I'm staying in a hotel near the forest. It is very warm and I go walking every day. There are lots of interesting museums here. The food is also wonderful.

Best wishes,

(Student's own name)

p.21 ex. 3
Answers
a   would like to see film; Friday or Saturday night?; time to meet; place to meet.
b   would like to come to party, bring a friend?; what records I could bring; what food I like.
c   number of brothers and sisters; names and ages of brothers and sisters; parents' jobs; where live.

Writing

p. 22 Spelling ex. 1
The correct spellings are friend, beautiful, Wednesday, having, bicycle, aeroplane, forty, families, which, address.

pp. 22-3 Spelling ex. 3
The misspelt words are friend, eighteen, quite, think, beautiful, which, clothes, meets, people, there, too, often, swimming, riding, bicycles, always, with, very.

p. 23 Punctuation ex. 1
Answers
a   Where can I find Mr John Smith, please?
b   My birthday is on Wednesday, the fourth of July.
c   She lives in the USA but her parents live in Spain and her husband's parents live in Singapore.
d   Rosemary has a beautiful, new, Japanese bicycle.
e   Can you speak Italian?
f   John's book is in his aunt's bag.

p. 23 Punctuation ex. 2
Answers
I come from Russia. The capital city of my country is Moscow. It's a very beautiful city with many old churches and many interesting new buildings too. I like Moscow best in winter. From November to March or April we have snow and you can ski in the parks or on the Lenin Hills beside the Moscow State University. There are many fine museums in Moscow and my favourite is the Tretyakov Gallery. My parents' flat is in the city centre and I can see the Kremlin from my bedroom window. Would you like to come and visit Moscow next year? You can stay at my parents' flat.

p. 24 Grammar ex. 1
Answers
I have two brothers and .... My sister works .....I live ....I am going .... My sister is a nurse and I want ... My sister plays ... but she doesn't play ... She can also swim ... My brothers don't swim well ....

p. 24 Grammar ex. 2
Answers
a in; b on; c at; d in; e at, - ; f in, to or - ; g between; h to; i on; j in; k on; l to; m to; n at; o of.

p. 25 Grammar ex. 5
Answers
There are .... My two brothers ... We were all born in July. ... and my mother is a teacher. We live in a small flat .... We speak to each other ... My mother cooks .... We are ....My brother usually does the washing-up.... We often go to the cinema .... I am always happy to go home ....

Model Compositions

p.25
Here are some suggested compositions on the titles set at the bottom of page 25. The compositions are of the length and complexity appropriate for Basic level. Note that they are only suggestions. Students may write completely different compositions that are at least as good, if not better, than the suggestions on page 14.

My Best Friend

My best friend's name is Sheila. She is sixteen years old. She has short, dark hair. She is short and slim. She loves animals, reading and music. Her favourite kind of music is Spanish flamenco music. She hasn't any brothers and sisters but she has a dog. Her dog is called Brandy. Sheila and I usually go for a walk with Brandy at the weekend.

My Family

My family is not very big. There are my parents, my brother and me. My father is a professor of geography and my mother is a housewife. My brother is older than I am. He is a student at university. He is studying zoology. His name is Duncan. I also have some cousins in the south of Scotland and in London. We usually visit them in the summer holidays.

The Capital City of My Country

I come from Scotland and the capital city of my country is Edinburgh. It is a beautiful city. There are many old buildings in Edinburgh. Its castle is very famous. Many tourists visit Edinburgh. There is a popular festival in this beautiful city at the end of the summer. Edinburgh is not far from the sea and the hills. I love Edinburgh and want to live there one day.

What I Do at the Weekend

I love the weekend. I don't get up early. I read in bed and then get up. I usually do my homework on Saturday mornings. In the afternoon I often go into town with my mother or my friend, Sheila. I like shopping. On Sundays we often go for a walk. Sometimes we go out in the car. The weekend goes very quickly.

Listening Scripts

N.B. The text which is not in italics should be read aloud.

Practice Test One

LISTENING TEST, PART ONE, PART ONE. *(Allow time to check that candidates have found PART 1.)*

Listen and match what you hear with one of the answers. For example, if you hear: It's nineteen kilometres, nineteen kilometres, the matching answer is C. Put a circle round your answer.

Number one, number one. *(10 seconds)*
   Her telephone number is oh–seven–one, six–three–five, one–three–eight–oh, that's oh–seven–one, six–three–five, one–three–eight–oh. *(10 seconds)*

Number two, number two. *(10 seconds)*
   Our train leaves at eleven forty, at eleven forty. *(10 seconds)*

Number three, number three. *(10 seconds)*
   Her name is Gill Jack, G-I- double L, J-A-C-K, G-I- double L, J-A-C-K. *(10 seconds)*

Number four, number four . *(10 seconds)*
   They're having a party on October the twenty fifth, October the twenty fifth. *(10 seconds)*

Number five, number five. *(10 seconds)*
   There is a small circle in the bottom left-hand corner of a large rectangle. There is a small circle in the bottom left-hand corner of a large rectangle. *(10 seconds)*

PART TWO, PART TWO. *(Allow time to check that candidates have found PART 2.)*

Choose the best reply to each sentence. For example, if you hear : 'Can you tell me the time?' the best answer is C - a quarter past two. Ready?

Number one, number one. *(10 seconds)*
   Do you like English?
   Do you like English? *(10 seconds)*

Number two, number two. *(10 seconds)*
   How much is this dog?
   How much is this dog? *(10 seconds)*

Number three, number three. *(10 seconds)*
   Where is the dictionary ?
   Where is the dictionary? *(10 seconds)*

Number four, number four. *(10 seconds)*
   Give me your pen.
   Give me your pen. *(10 seconds)*

Number five, number five. *(10 seconds)*
   I'm going to New York on Saturday.
   I'm going to New York on Saturday. *(10 seconds)*

PART THREE, PART THREE. *(Allow time to check that candidates have found PART 3.)*

You are going to complete a table. The table gives some information about holidays. Look at the table. Some information is given to help you. *(15 seconds for looking at the diagram.)* Listen to the instructions. You will hear the information **twice**. Ready? *(Allow 10 seconds between each instruction.)*

Write 'Cost' at the top of the last column. Write 'Cost' at the top of the last column.
Write 'Place' at the top of the second column. Write 'Place' at the top of the second column.
The Paris holiday is for four days and costs £200. The Paris holiday is for four days and costs £200.
The most expensive holiday is the one in Bangkok. It costs £1,100. It costs £1,100.
The fourteen day holiday is in Fiji. The fourteen day holiday is in Fiji.
Holiday number four is three days in Cairo. Holiday number four is three days in Cairo.
The holiday in Fiji costs £999. The holiday in Fiji costs £999.
The Bangkok holiday is for twelve days. The Bangkok holiday is for twelve days.

Now listen again - ready? *(Repeat the instructions.)*

(Wait 30 seconds before going on to PART 4.)

PART FOUR, PART FOUR. (Allow time to check that candidates have found PART 4.)

Look at the map. (30 seconds) Now listen and mark Elizabeth's house, her school, the cinema and Mary's house. Also mark the walk which Elizabeth takes with her dog. You will hear the information **twice**. Ready?

Hello, my name is Elizabeth. I live on Park Street beside the park. I like living beside a park. I play there nearly every day. My school is near too. To get to school I turn left when I come out of my house. I walk along Park Street until I come to Mill Lane. I turn left into Mill Lane and my school is on the right-hand side of the road opposite a church. My school is called St Margaret's - just like the church. There is a cinema next door to the school. Sometimes we go to the cinema after school. My friend Mary lives near to the school too. She lives in Bell Road between the bank and the post office. Mary and I often go for a walk in the evening with my dog. We always take the same walk. Mary comes to my house and we go straight into the park. We walk across the park to a shop called The Sweet Shop. You can buy very good ice cream there. Then we walk along Hyde Lane and we turn right into Mill Lane. We walk past the cinema and our school and we then turn right at the end of the road into Park Street. We come back to my house and listen to some records. Then Mary goes home. It is a very nice way to spend an evening.

Now listen again. Ready? (Read the instructions again.)

(45 seconds)

You now have 1 hour 40 minutes to complete the rest of the paper.

Practice Test Two

LISTENING TEST, PART ONE, PART ONE. (Allow time to check that candidates have found PART 1.)

Listen and match what you hear with one of the answers. For example, if you hear: It's nineteen kilometres, nineteen kilometres, the matching answer is C. Put a circle round your answer.

Number one, number one. (10 seconds)
    Come here at ten to nine, ten to nine. (10 seconds)

Number two, number two. (10 seconds)
    It's the twenty-sixth of June, the twenty-sixth of June. (10 seconds)

Number three, number three. (10 seconds)
    His name is Andrews, that's A-N-D-R-E-W-S, A-N-D-R-E-W-S. (10 seconds)

Number four, number four. (10 seconds)
    Her handbag is in front of the chair, her handbag is in front of the chair. (10 seconds)

Number five, number five. (10 seconds)
    His telephone number is two-four, double three, six-seven. His telephone number is two-four, double three, six-seven. (10 seconds)

PART TWO, PART TWO. (Allow time to check that candidates have found PART 2.)

Choose the best reply to each sentence. For example, if you hear: 'Can you tell me the time?' the best answer is C - a quarter past two. Ready?

Number one, number one. (10 seconds)
    Would you like some sugar?
    Would you like some sugar? (10 seconds)

Number two, number two. (10 seconds)
    What's her name?
    What's her name? (10 seconds)

Number three, number three. (10 seconds)
    Is that your book?
    Is that your book? (10 seconds)

Number four, number four. (10 seconds)
    Mary's got a new job.
    Mary's got a new job. (10 seconds)

Number five, number five. (10 seconds)
    Does John live with his uncle?
    Does John live with his uncle? (10 seconds)

PART THREE, PART THREE. (Allow time to check that candidates have found PART 3.)

You are going to complete a table. The table gives some information about cars. Look at the table. (15 *seconds for looking at the table.)* Listen to the instructions. You will hear the information **twice.** Ready? *(Allow 10 seconds between each instruction.)*

Write 'Cars' above the table. Write 'Cars' above the table.
Write 'Cost' at the top of the last column. Write 'Cost' at the top of the last column.
Car number 2 is red. Car number 2 is red.
The third car costs eight thousand pounds. The third car costs eight thousand pounds.
The green car is German. The green car is German.
The licence number of the last car is DCA 549G. The licence number of the last car is DCA 549G.
The Japanese car is two years old. The Japanese car is two years old.
Now listen again - ready? *(Repeat the instructions.)*

(Wait 30 seconds before going on to PART 4.)

PART FOUR, PART FOUR. *(Allow time to check that candidates have found PART 4.)*

Look at the form. *(30 seconds)* Now listen and fill in the form. You will hear the information **twice.** Ready?

Hello, my name is Jan, Jan Higgins, that's J-A-N, H-I-G-G-I-N-S.
I come from a very large family. I've got two brothers and three sisters. I'm the youngest.
I'm English and I'm thirty years old. My birthday is the tenth of October.
I live in Oxford at 47 Long Road. I live in a small house with a large garden. I'm a teacher. I teach French at a school for girls. I like my job very much. Every year I go to France with twenty or thirty of my students and we usually have a very interesting time there.
I am married and I have one daughter. Her name is Nathalie. She is seven years old and goes to the school where I work. My husband's name is Tony and he's a bus driver. He drives Nathalie and me to school every day.

(Wait 30 seconds before the second reading.)

Now listen again. Ready? *(Read the instructions again.)*

(45 seconds)

You now have 1 hour 40 minutes to complete the rest of the paper.

Practice Test Three

LISTENING TEST, PART ONE, PART ONE. *(Allow time to check that candidates have found PART 1.)*

Listen and match what you hear with one of the answers. For example, if you hear: It's nineteen kilometres, nineteen kilometres, the matching answer is C. Put a circle round your answer.

Number one, number one. *(10 seconds)*
   Her telephone number is double three-oh-nine-one, double three-oh-nine-one *(10 seconds)*

Number two, number two. *(10 seconds)*

His name is Jeffrey Stone, that's J-E-double-F-R-E-Y, S-T-O-N-E, that's J-E-double-F-R-E-Y, S-T-O-N-E. *(10 seconds)*

Number three, number three. *(10 seconds)*

Please come at quarter past six, at quarter past six. *(10 seconds)*

Number four, number four. *(10 seconds)*
   The meeting is on the twenty-fourth of February, the twenty-fourth of February. *(10 seconds)*

Number five, number five. *(10 seconds)*
   Her house is at the end of the road on the left-hand side.
   Her house is at the end of the road on the left-hand side. *(10 seconds)*

PART TWO, PART TWO. *(Allow time to check that candidates have found PART 2.)*

Choose the best reply to each sentence. For example, if you hear: 'Can you tell me the time?' the best answer is C - a quarter past two. Ready?

Number one, number one. *(10 seconds)*
   How much is a cup of coffee?
   How much is a cup of coffee? *(10 seconds)*

Number two, number two. *(10 seconds)*
How old are you?
How old are you? *(10 seconds)*

Number three, number three. *(10 seconds)*
Can you help me, please?
Can you help me, please? *(10 seconds)*

Number four, number four. *(10 seconds)*
I'd like an ice cream.
I'd like an ice cream. *(10 seconds)*

Number five, number five. *(10 seconds)*
Is that her coat?
Is that her coat? *(10 seconds)*

PART THREE, PART THREE. *(Allow time to check that candidates have found PART 3.)*

You are going to complete a table. The table gives some information about aeroplanes. Look at the table. Some information is given to help you. *(15 seconds for looking at the table.)* Listen to the instructions. You will hear the information **twice**.

Ready? *(Allow 10 seconds between each instruction.)*

Write 'aeroplanes' above the table. Write 'aeroplanes' above the table.
The first aeroplane is going to Moscow. The first aeroplane is going to Moscow.
The Singapore plane is flight number KL 235. The Singapore plane is flight number KL 235.
Flight number NZ 445 leaves at 10.30. Flight number NZ 445 leaves at 10.30.
The plane which leaves at 12 o'clock is flight number SU 897. The plane which leaves at 12 o'clock is flight number SU 897.
Flight AF 213 leaves at 16.30. Flight AF 213 leaves at 16.30.
The New York plane leaves at 15.20. The New York plane leaves at 15.20.
The last plane is going to Paris. The last plane is going to Paris.
Now listen again - ready? *(Repeat the instructions.)*

(Wait 30 seconds before going on to PART 4.)

PART FOUR, PART FOUR. *(Allow time to check that candidates have found PART 4.)*

Look at the form. *(30 seconds)* Now listen and fill in the form. You will hear the information **twice.** Ready?

Hello, I'm Tony Robb, that's T-O-N-Y, R-O-double B. I live in Switzerland now.
I was born on the thirtieth of October, 1960. I wasn't born in Switzerland. I was born in London. I'm English.
I'm married. I've been married for four years. I've got one child, a little boy. His name's Tom and he's two years old. He was born on the twenty-first of March.
I work in a hotel in Switzerland. I'm a hotel manager. I speak French and German and, of course, English. I love languages. In our hotel we have many visitors from different countries.

(Wait 30 seconds before the second reading.)

Now listen again. Ready? *(Read the instructions again.)*

(45 seconds)

You now have 1 hour 40 minutes to complete the rest of the paper.

Practice Test Four

LISTENING TEST, PART ONE, PART ONE. *(Allow time to check that candidates have found PART 1.)*

Listen and match what you hear with one of the answers. For example, if you hear: It's nineteen kilometres, nineteen kilometres, the matching answer is C. Put a circle round your answer.

Number one, number one. *(10 seconds)*
Her birthday is the twelfth of May.
Her birthday is the twelfth of May. *(10 seconds)*

Number two, number two. *(10 seconds)*
My telephone number is two six four, double oh nine.
My telephone number is two six four, double oh nine. *(10 seconds)*

Number three, number three. *(10 seconds)*
 The film starts at three twenty.
 The film starts at three twenty. *(10 seconds)*

Number four, number four. *(10 seconds)*
 My mother's name is Queenie Barlow, that's Q-U-double-E-N-I-E, B-A-R-L-O-W.
 My mother's name is Queenie Barlow, that's Q-U-double-E-N-I-E, B-A-R-L-O-W.

(10 seconds)

Number five, number five . *(10 seconds)*
 The cinema is next to the Post Office.
 The cinema is next to the Post Office. *(10 seconds)*

PART TWO, PART TWO. *(Allow time to check that candidates have found PART 2.)*

Choose the best reply to each sentence. For example, if you hear: 'Can you tell me the time?' the best answer is C - a quarter past two. Ready?

Number one, number one. *(10 seconds)*
 Where do you live?
 Where do you live? *(10 seconds)*

Number two, number two. *(10 seconds)*
 Do you know Mary?
 Do you know Mary? *(10 seconds)*

Number three, number three. *(10 seconds)*
 How are you?
 How are you? *(10 seconds)*

Number four, number four. *(10 seconds)*
 I like him very much but I'm not sure about her.
 I like him very much but I'm not sure about her.
(10 seconds)

Number five, number five. *(10 seconds)*
 Has John got any brothers or sisters?
 Has John got any brothers or sisters? *(10 seconds)*

PART THREE, PART THREE. *(Allow time to check that candidates have found PART 3.)*

This part is about a group of three foreign students who are in England learning English. Look at the table. The column on the left gives the students' names. The other columns give more information about the students. Some words are given to help you. *(15 seconds for looking at the table.)* Complete the table. Listen to the instructions. You will hear the information **twice.**

Ready? *(Allow 10 seconds between each instruction.)*

Write 'Nationality' at the top of the second column. Write 'Nationality' at the top of the second column. Write 'Age' at the top of the last column. Write 'Age' at the top of the last column.
The first student is German. The first student is German.
The Brazilian student is a mechanic. The Brazilian student is a mechanic.
Yumiko is Japanese. Yumiko is Japanese.
Roberto is 23. Roberto is 23.
Hans is 21. Hans is 21.
The university student is 19. The university student is 19.

Now listen again - ready? *(Repeat the instructions.)*

(Wait 30 seconds before going on to PART 4.)

PART FOUR, PART FOUR. *(Allow time to check that candidates have found PART 4.)*

Look at the form. *(30 seconds)* Now listen and fill in the form. You will hear the information **twice.** Ready?

Good morning. My name is Kim Smart, that's K-I-M, S-M-A-R-T. Kim is an unusual name, I know, but I like it.
I was born on the sixth of February 1965. My older sister was also born on the sixth of February but she is two years older than me. I was born in New York but I am British. My parents are both British but my father had a job in the States when I was born.
I am married. I got married two years ago. We haven't got any children yet but we would like to have children one day.
I work in a restaurant. I'm a cook. I like my job very much but the hours are not very good. I work every evening from six to eleven.

(Wait 30 seconds before the second reading.)

Now listen again. Ready?

(Read the instructions again.)

(45 seconds)

You now have 1 hour 40 minutes to complete the rest of the paper.

Practice Test Five

LISTENING TEST, PART ONE, PART ONE. *(Allow time to check that candidates have found PART 1.)*

Listen and match what you hear with one of the answers. For example, if you hear: It's nineteen kilometres, nineteen kilometres, the matching answer is C. Put a circle round your answer.

Number one, number one. *(10 seconds)*
He lives at thirty-six Blinco Road, that's thirty-six B-L-I-N-C-O, R-O-A-D, that's thirty-six B-L-I-N-C-O, R-O-A-D. *(10 seconds)*

Number two, number two. *(10 seconds)*
The time is now twenty to four.
The time is now twenty to four. *(10 seconds)*

Number three, number three. *(10 seconds)*
Your glasses are on the table.
Your glasses are on the table. *(10 seconds)*

Number four, number four. *(10 seconds)*
Phone me on double six three, oh four nine.
Phone me on double six three, oh four nine. *(10 seconds)*

Number five, number five. *(10 seconds)*
The concert is on the thirteenth of November.
The concert is on the thirteenth of November. *(10 seconds)*

PART TWO, PART TWO. *(Allow time to check that candidates have found PART 2.)*

Choose the best reply to each sentence. For example, if you hear:'Can you tell me the time?' the best answer is C - a quarter past two. Ready?

Number one, number one. *(10 seconds)*
Can I help you?
Can I help you? *(10 seconds)*

Number two, number two. *(10 seconds)*
Are you English?
Are you English? *(10 seconds)*

Number three, number three. *(10 seconds)*
Is there a telephone here?
Is there a telephone here? *(10 seconds)*

Number four, number four. *(10 seconds)*
I'll see you at six o'clock.
I'll see you at six o'clock. *(10 seconds)*

Number five, number five. *(10 seconds)*
Is that Mary's brother?
Is that Mary's brother? *(10 seconds)*

PART THREE, PART THREE. *(Allow time to check that candidates have found PART 3.)*

You are going to complete a table. The table is about different houses.

Look at the table. Some words are given to help you. *(15 seconds for looking at the table.)* Complete the table. Listen to the instructions.

You will hear the information **twice**. Ready? *(Allow 10 seconds between each instruction.)*

Write 'Houses' below the table. Write 'Houses' below the table.
Write 'Bedrooms' at the top of the third column. Write 'Bedrooms' at the top of the third column.
Write 'Living-rooms' at the top of the fourth column. Write 'Living-rooms' at the top of the fourth column.
The second house has got a garden. The second house has got a garden.
The fourth house has got six bedrooms. The fourth house has got six bedrooms.
The first house has three bedrooms. The first house has three bedrooms
The second house has two living-rooms. The second house has two living-rooms.
The third house has four bedrooms. The third house has four bedrooms.
Now listen again - ready? *(Repeat the instructions.)*

(Wait 30 seconds before going on to PART 4.)

PART FOUR, PART FOUR. *(Allow time to check that candidates have found PART 4.)*

Look at the shopping list. *(30 seconds)* Now listen and complete the shopping list. You will hear the information **twice.** Ready?

Could you please buy me some things when you are in town today. I need a kilo of apples, please. One kilo of apples. I'd also like five bananas so I can make a fruit salad. We need potatoes too. Could you get three kilos of potatoes, please. Oh, and we must have some milk. Two bottles will be fine. Could you also get two boxes of chocolates - one for Mrs Smith, who's in hospital, and one for Jane for her birthday. That's two nice boxes of chocolates. Oh, I nearly forgot. Sugar. Could you get me a one kilo packet of sugar. Finally, could you get me a black pen. It must be black. Thanks very much. Here's ten pounds. I hope that's enough.

(Wait 30 seconds before the second reading.)

Now listen again. Ready? *(Read the instructions again.)*

(45 seconds)

You now have 1 hour 40 minutes to complete the rest of the paper.

Answers to Practice Tests

Practice Test One

Listening

Part 1
1 C
2 D
3 B
4 B
5 A

Part 2
1 C
2 D
3 C
4 A
5 D

Part 3

Holiday number	Place	Number of days	Cost
1	Fiji	14	£999
2	Paris	4	£200
3	Bangkok	12	£1,100
4	Cairo	3	£388

Part 4

See map.
Elizabeth's house is on Park Street beside the park.
The school is on Mill Lane opposite the church.
The cinema is the building beside the school.
Mary's house is the house on Bell Lane between the bank and the post office.
Elizabeth and Mary's walk starts at Elizabeth's house, goes across the park to the sweet shop, comes out of the sweet shop and turns right into Hyde Lane, turns right into Mill Lane and then turns right into Park Street. It ends up back at Elizabeth's house.

English Usage

1 years
2 with
3 in
4 do
5 but
6 doing
7 is
8 much
9 at
10 play

Reading One

1 C
2 A
3 D
4 C
5 B

Reading Two

The pictures should be numbered as follows 2; 7; 3; 6; 4; 5.

Reading Three

The houses should be named from left to right Shop; Brown; Grey; Black; White; Green.

Reading and Writing

There are many different ways of answering this question. Here is one possibility.

Dear Jan,

Thank you for your letter. This is my typical day. I usually get up at half past seven. I wash and dress and have my breakfast at eight o'clock. I walk to school. I get to school at nine o'clock and lessons start at nine fifteen. We have lunch at school at half past twelve. School finishes at four o'clock. I walk home with my friends. I have my evening meal at six o'clock. In the evenings I do my homework, read and watch television. I go to bed at ten o'clock. On Saturdays and Sundays I don't go to school. I get up later and I go to bed later. I often play tennis with my friend, Anne. Sometimes I go to a party on Saturdays. What about you? What is a typical day for you?

With all good wishes,

Felicity

Writing

No model answers are given for this or for any other of the Writing questions in the Practice Tests. For an idea of the length and the complexity of the compositions expected of the best students at this level, see the model compositions provided at the end of the Basic Exam Help section.

Practice Test Two

Listening

Part 1	Part 2
1 B	1 C
2 B	2 A
3 C	3 D
4 C	4 B
5 B	5 C

Part 3

Cars

Car	Colour	Nationality	Licence Number	Age	<u>Cost</u>
1	green	<u>German</u>	EFL 261D	4 years old	£9,900
2	<u>red</u>	Italian	PRT 472A	7 years old	£6,750
3	black	British	DLR 338B	6 years old	<u>£8,000</u>
4	white	Japanese	<u>DCA 549G</u>	<u>2 years old</u>	£5,500

Part 4

Higgins; Jan; English; 30; 47 Long Road, Oxford;
Teacher; Married; One

English Usage

1	in	6	but
2	They	7	we
3	by	8	there
4	for	9	It
5	too	10	am

Reading One

1 C; 2 B; 3 B; 4 C; 5 A.

Reading Two

The following points should be added to the table,
going from top to bottom:
play football
11%
play with computers
25%
read (magazines or books)
60%
play with an animal
78%
84%
watch television

Reading Three

Forest Glade School; 250 pupils; 20 teachers; Miss
Jones; No; Yes; Glade station; 9.15; 3.30.

Reading and Writing

Dear Jane,

I am having a lovely holiday in London. I am staying in
a hotel near the city centre. It is very warm and I go
sightseeing every day. There are lots of interesting
museums in London. The food here is also good.
See you soon,
(Student's own name)
(Address as on model postcard in test.)

Writing

No model answers are given for this or for any other of
the Writing questions in the Practice Tests. For an idea
of the length and the complexity of the compositions
expected of the best students at this level, see the model
compositions provided at the end of the Basic Exam
Help section.

Practice Test Three

Listening

Part 1		Part 2	
1	C	1	A
2	D	2	C
3	C	3	B
4	B	4	D
5	A	5	B

Part 3

Aeroplanes

Flight Number	Going to	Leaving at
SU 897	Moscow	12.00
KL 235	Singapore	14.15
NZ 445	Auckland	10.30
US 643	New York	15.20
AF 213	Paris	16.30

Part 4

Tony Robb; 30th October 1960; Married; one; two years old; English; hotel manager; French, German, English.

English Usage

1	to	6	very
2	are	7	an
3	in	8	is
4	and	9	I
5	do	10	my

Reading One

1 C; 2 A; 3 C; 4 B; 5 D.

Reading Two

The dotted line should start at the 'You are here' marker and should go along the edge of the park, turning right into Park Street and then left into Hope Street, finishing up at the second building from the end on the left (between the school and the art gallery).

Reading Three

Johnson; Mary and Jack; 2; Peter (age 10) and Mark (age 8); 27 Main Street, London; policeman; secretary; Ford.

Reading and Writing

The answers to this question will depend totally on the students' personal details. It is not, therefore, useful to give a model answer.

Writing

No model answers are given for this or for any other of the Writing questions in the Practice Tests. For an idea of the length and the complexity of the compositions expected of the best students at this level, see the model compositions provided at the end of the Basic Exam Help section.

Listening

Part 1
1 B
2 A
3 C
4 C
5 B

Part 2
1 B
2 A
3 C
4 B
5 C

Part 3

Name	Nationality	Occupation	Age
Hans	German	bus driver	21
Roberto	Brazilian	mechanic	23
Yumiko	Japanese	university student	19

Part 4
Smart; Kim; 6th February 1965 New York; British; married; none; cook.

English Usage

1 and
2 to
3 a
4 works
5 with
6 has
7 in
8 there
9 are
10 the

Reading One

1 C; 2 B; 3 A; 4 D; 5 B.

Reading Two

The pictures should be numbered in the following order – 2; 8; 6; 5; 3; 7.

Reading Three

The shirt should have Peter on the label; the pen should be labelled Rose; the sunglasses should be labelled Anna; the photography book should be labelled Aunt Cecilia; the Dire Straits record should be labelled Janet. The labels on the skirt, swimming costume, crayons and Beethoven cassette should be left blank.

Reading and Writing

Dear Jo,

I hope you can come to a party on Saturday April 12th. It is my brother's birthday. Come at 7.30. Take the number 8 bus and get off at the stop beside the Rock Hotel. Turn right at the lights and our house is next to the school. We are looking forward to seeing you then.

  With best wishes,

  (Student's own name)

Writing

No model answers are given for this or for any other of the Writing questions in the Practice Tests. For an idea of the length and the complexity of the compositions expected of the best students at this level, see the model compositions provided at the end of the Basic Exam Help section.

Practice Test Five

Listening

Part 1	Part 2
1 D	1 B
2 D	2 D
3 A	3 A
4 C	4 D
5 A	5 C

Part 3

House Number	Garden	<u>Bedrooms</u>	<u>Living-rooms</u>
1	No	<u>3</u>	2
2	<u>Yes</u>	3	<u>2</u>
3	Yes	<u>4</u>	3
4	2	<u>6</u>	4

<u>Houses</u>

Part 4

1 kilo apples; 5 bananas; 3 kilos potatoes; 2 bottles of milk; 2 boxes of chocolates; 1 kilo sugar; 1 black pen.

English Usage

1	can	6	by
2	Many	7	of
3	There	8	to
4	have	9	often
5	go	10	live

Reading One

1 C; 2 B; 3 B; 4 D; 5 B.

Reading Two

English is the first lesson on Monday; Biology is the lesson after lunch on Tuesday; Physical Education is the last lesson on Wednesday; Geography is the lesson before lunch on Thursday; Chemistry is the lesson after lunch on Thursday; Music is the last lesson on Friday.

Reading Three

The pictures should be named in the following order from left to right – John Wright; blank; Penny Jolly; blank; Mary Jolly; Jim Stokes; blank; Paul Stokes.

Reading and Writing

There are many different ways of answering this question. Here is one possibility.

There are two windows in the room. My bed is next to one window. There is a table beside my bed. There is a vase of flowers on the table. I also have a chair, a bookcase, a wardrobe and a record-player. There is a picture on the wall above the record-player.

Writing

No model answers are given for this or for any other of the Writing questions in the Practice Tests. For an idea of the length and the complexity of the compositions expected of the best students at this level, see the model compositions provided at the end of the Basic Exam Help section.

Pitman ESOL Practice Tests – Elementary Level

Exam Help

Listening

p. 7 ex. 1
Personal details for dictation
Gerry Gilliatt   47   Flat 54B, 8 Smayle Square,
Cirencester   0874 21105
Jeanette Bing   28   756 Hadley Gardens, Bayview
06385 24563
Gail Ellison   30   29 Jerome Crescent, Quexton
0758 443109

p. 7 ex. 4
Suggestion for picture dictation
Take a blank piece of paper. In the middle of the paper draw a rectangle. In the rectangle draw a small picture of a car. In the top left-hand corner of your page draw a small circle. In the other three corners draw a small triangle. Above the rectangle write the word BARGAIN. Below the rectangle, write ONLY £500.

p. 8 ex. 6
Answers

What time is it?	Half past six.
How old is your sister?	Ten.
What's your friend's name?	Jim Parker.
Are you Spanish?	No, I'm not.
Can you play the guitar?	Yes, I can.
Is he a student?	No, a teacher.
How are you?	Fine, thanks.
Where do you come from?	Athens.
What's your favourite book?	My English dictionary.
How much does it cost?	Six pounds fifty.
Do you take sugar in coffee?	No, I don't.
Is this book yours?	No, it isn't.

p. 8 ex. 7
Answers
he's; we aren't or we're not; I can't; she won't; we shan't; she's had.

p. 8 ex. 9
Answers
Possible responses to each of the statements:
So did I!; No, it isn't; Shall I close the window?;
There's a cafe over there; No, it isn't; Yes, of course.
What can I do?

p. 8 ex. 10
Text to read to the students. (Read each text twice.)
a I'm afraid there are a number of things that I'd be really grateful if you could do for me while you're staying in the flat. First, could you please return my library book to the central library. You'll find the book on the kitchen table. Then could you water the plants in my bedroom – once a week is quite enough and not too much water, please. Could you also cut the grass once a week. It should only take you about twenty minutes as the garden is so small. When you go out every day, leave a light on in the house. My mother always says that it stops burglars taking an unhealthy interest in the place. I hope she's right. Finally, don't give my holiday address or phone number to anyone else. Only you and my family know where I am and that's how I'd like it to stay. I want to have a month of total peace. Thanks a lot. See you next month.

b If there are any problems while I'm away, contact my brother-in-law. His name's Garry, that's G-A-double R-Y, Pierce, that's P-I-E-R-C-E, not E-A as some people spell it, I think. He lives quite near here in a village called Boxbridge, that's B-O-X and then bridge spelt as usual. There's a little stream there called the Box and it's really very pretty. He and my sister live there at 10 Pond Lane, that's P-O-N-D, of course, number 10. They haven't got a phone at home but you could ring him at work on 071 658 9991.

c If you want to get to Glasgow by the evening, you'll have to catch the 2.30 train at the latest. It takes almost five hours. Let me just check, yes, you get in at 6.55. You need to change just once, that's at Peterborough, that's P-E-T-E-R-B-O-R-O-U-G-H. That's only about thirty minutes from here.

Answers

a return library book, water plants in bedroom, cut grass, leave light on, don't give address or phone number to anyone.
b Garry Pierce, 10 Pond Lane, Boxbridge, 071 658 9991.
c 2.30, 6.55, Peterborough.

p. 9 ex. 11
Text to read to the students.
You are at the bus station. Come out of the bus station into Long Road and walk south along that road. Take the second turning on the left. That's High Street. Walk quite a long way along High Street. You'll pass a park on your left. Take the second road on your left after the park. Where are you?
Answer: Old Street.

English Usage

p. 10 ex. 1
Answers
verb go; adjective beautiful; adverb quickly; preposition on; conjunction but; article a; pronoun we.

p. 10 ex. 2
Answers
b preposition; c verb; d adverb; e article; f noun; g pronoun; h conjunction.

p. 11 ex. 3
Answers
b by; c go; d well; e the; f fly; g I; h and.

p. 11 ex. 4
Answers

1	him	6	very	11	in
2	went	7	there	12	they
3	met	8	ago	13	could
4	to	9	it	14	back
5	where	10	much	15	next

p. 12
Answers

1	not	6	for	11	every
2	in	7	than	12	sleep
3	hard	8	time	13	are
4	it	9	when	14	as
5	to	10	lasts	15	they

p. 13
Answers

1	largest	6	with	11	by
2	very	7	for	12	In
3	than	8	are	13	between
4	only	9	called	14	Since
5	is	10	as	15	both

Reading One

pp. 14-15 ex. 1
Answers
C; B; B; C; D.

pp. 15-16 ex. 2
Answers
a she had a bad attack of flu.
b There are gentle hills all round them and a river runs through their fields.
c Let's celebrate one evening soon.
d when they woke up, it was pouring with rain.
e the heart, the lungs and the digestive system.

Reading Two

p. 16 ex. 1
Answers
The girl is wearing a striped shirt, a skirt with a belt, a bracelet, socks and shoes. The man is wearing a suit (jacket and trousers), a hat, glasses, a shirt and tie and shoes. He is carrying a coat, a newspaper and an umbrella.

p.17 ex. 2

There are many different ways of answering this exercise. Here are some possible sentences using the prepositions under the picture.

There are some books on the desk.
There is a waste-paper basket beside the desk.
There are some flowers in a vase.
The chair is near the desk.
The stereo is next to the bookcase.
The armchair is behind the girl.
The man is lying opposite the girl.
The girl is in front of the armchair.
There is a picture above the bed.
The stereo is below the window.
There is a rug under the bed.
The cat is between the chair and the waste-paper basket.
There are some letters on the right-hand side of the desk.
The vase of flowers is on the top of the bookcase.
The rug is in the middle of the room.
The wardrobe is in the corner of the room.

p. 18 ex. 3
Answers
B; C; A; Jane – A and E; Philip – F and G; Simon – C and D; Anna – B and H.

Reading Three

pp. 19-20
Answers
1 North America; bigger; 25 centimetres.
2 1871; Alexandra; Aleksey.
3 2,000; 1,400,000 kilometres; 6,000° Centigrade; once every 25 days.
4 Mexico and La Gomera; men; 8 kilometres.
5 1896; 1908; 27 years; 15 million.

Reading and Writing

pp.21-22 ex. 1
Suggested answer

Dear Pat,

Thank you for your letter. I am fourteen years old too. I live with my family in a flat in the north of London. I have one brother and one sister. I am the oldest. My father works in a bank and my mother is a secretary. I have short fair hair and am quite tall. I love football but I don't play very well. I also love going to the cinema and to the theatre. There are lots of good cinemas and theatres in London. Please write again soon. Tell me what your school is like.

With best wishes,

    (Student's own name)

pp.22-23 ex. 2
Suggested answer
Get off the bus at the bus station. Turn right into Station Street. Walk past the railway station. Turn left at the roundabout just past the railway station. Then take the first turning on your right. Walk along that street until you come to the George Hotel. It's on a corner on the left-hand side of the road. Turn left just before the George Hotel. Duke Street is then the first street on the right. Our house, number 31, is on the left-hand side of the road. You can't miss it.

p.23 ex. 3
The four things that must be mentioned are:
a where you live; who you live with; what you like doing in your spare time; a description of a typical day for you.
b what the weather is like in your country in summer; what to see in capital city; where else to visit (apart from capital city); what souvenirs of your country to buy.
c what you did on last holiday; who you were with; where you stayed; the food.

p.23 ex. 3

Suggested answers

a I live with my parents in a small town in Scotland. In my spare time I read a lot and I also go riding. On a typical day I ride for an hour before school. I go to school from nine to four. After school I do my homework and then sometimes go riding again. I read a lot in the evenings and also watch television.

b The weather is warm and dry in my country in the summer. There are lots of interesting museums and art galleries in the capital city. The theatres are also very good. If you have time, you must go to the beach. The mountains in the north are very beautiful too. Clothes and wooden toys are good souvenirs, I think.

c On my last holiday I went to France with my friend, Anne, and her parents. We camped and stayed on a camp-site in the mountains. We had a marvellous time. It was very hot and did not rain once. We climbed some mountains and went canoeing. The food was fantastic. Sometimes we cooked at the camp-site but usually we ate in restaurants.

Writing

p. 24 ex. 1

Correct spellings are – wonderful; Sunday; which; paid; bike; weather; fifteen; beautifully; believe; necessary; worries; different; beginning.

p. 25 Punctuation ex. 1

Answers

a Where did you learn to speak Portuguese?
b The meeting is at the Royal Hotel on Thursday the eighth of August.
c I've never been to the USSR but I'd love to go there one day.
d 'Where has John gone?' asked Annette.
e Mark has just bought a lovely, red, Italian sports car.
f I'm using Mary's pen because I've lost mine.
g The National Art Gallery is in Trafalgar Square.
h 'Speak more slowly, please', asked Sandra.

p. 25 Grammar ex.

Answers

1 We go .. 2 They visited ... 3 Did you go or Are you going ... 4 I was watching ... the phone rang. 5 John loves going... 6 Margaret very much wanted ... when she was .... 7 Do you know ... 8 ...I took ... I flew ... to visit my aunt.

p. 26 Prepositions

Answers

1 in, in; 2 in (on); 3 at; 4 at, in; 5 to; 6 by, by; 7 for, in; 8 on; 9 at; 10 - (to); 11 at; 12 in, with; 13 on; 14 in.

p. 26 What the Question asks you to do, ex. 1

The composition will not get a good mark because it has nothing to do with the title.

Suggested Compositions

p.26

There are many ways of writing a good composition on this subject. Here are two good compositions. They suggest the length and degree of complexity which a student at this level might aim at.

I enjoyed my first day at school. I was five years old. My mother took me to school and we met the teacher. Her name was Miss Dron. Then my mother said goodbye and I cried a little. There were twenty-five other girls there too. Miss Dron read us a story and then we learned a song. Then I painted a picture. At eleven o'clock we had some milk and a biscuit. Miss Dron played the piano and we danced a little. My mother came at twelve o'clock and we talked all afternoon about school.

My first day at secondary school was dreadful. I was new in the town and did not know any other children in my class. Nobody spoke to me. The first lesson was maths and all the other children knew the answers. I could not understand anything. The teacher gave us a lot of homework. We never had homework in my old school. That day was the longest day in my life. But on the way home I talked to another boy in my class. He lived in the next street to me. We decided to go to school together. I had a new friend. The next day school was all right.

Listening Scripts

N.B. *The text which is not in italics should be read aloud.*
Read at normal reading speed.

Practice Test One

LISTENING TEST, PART ONE, PART ONE. *(Allow time to check that candidates have found PART 1.)*

In this first part you will hear five sentences. Match each sentence with one of those written on your answer sheet. First look at the example. If you hear: 'The population is one hundred thousand, one hundred thousand' the matching answer is C. Put a circle round your answer.

Now listen. I will read the important part of each sentence twice.

Number one, number one. *(6 seconds)*
    Her phone number is oh-two, four-two-four, five-seven-eight-six, oh-two, four-two-four, five-seven-eight-six. *(10 seconds)*

Number two, number two. *(6 seconds)*
    They live in Shrewsbury. That's S-H-R-E-W-S-B-U-R-Y, S-H-R-E-W-S-B-U-R-Y.

(10 seconds)

Number three, number three. *(6 seconds)*
    There are two trees behind their house.
    There are two trees behind their house. *(10 seconds)*

Number four, number four. *(6 seconds)*
    My aunt's arriving on the twenty-eighth of March, the twenty-eighth of March. *(10 seconds)*

Number five, number five. *(6 seconds)*
    There's a small triangle in the centre of a large circle.
    There's a small triangle in the centre of a large circle. *(10 seconds)*

PART TWO, PART TWO. *(Check that candidates have found PART 2.)*

I'm going to read five sentences. Choose the best reply for each. Look at the example. If you hear: 'What time is it? What time is it?' the best answer is C. Put a circle round your answer.

Listen.

Number one, number one. *(6 seconds)*
    What's fourteen plus three?
    What's fourteen plus three? *(10 seconds)*

Number two, number two. *(6 seconds)*
    Will you have a cake?
    Will you have a cake? *(10 seconds)*

Number three, number three.' *(6 seconds)*
    How's your sister?
    How's your sister? *(10 seconds)*

Number four, number four. *(6 seconds)*
    How much is it?
    How much is it? *(10 seconds)*

Number five, number five. *(6 seconds)*
    Can you tell me where the post office is, please?
    Can you tell me where the post office is, please?
(10 seconds)

PART THREE, PART THREE. *(Check that candidates have found PART 3.)*

You are going to complete a chart. Look at the chart which gives some information about the five brothers and sisters in the Naunton family. *(15 seconds for looking at the page)* Listen to the instructions and complete the chart. There are some words under the chart to help you. You will hear the information **twice**.

Ready? *(Allow 10 seconds between each instruction.)*

Write The Naunton Family above the chart. Write The Naunton Family above the chart.
Listen to the following and write in the ages.
Roy is thirty. Roy is thirty.
Leo is twenty-six. Leo is twenty-six.
Robert is twenty-five. Robert is twenty-five.
Sue is twenty-three. Sue is twenty-three.
Now listen to the following and write in the jobs.
Sue, the only daughter, is a scientist. Sue, the only daughter, is a scientist.
Guy, the second oldest brother, is a dentist. Guy, the second oldest brother, is a dentist.
Leo is a zookeeper. Leo is a zookeeper.
Robert is a chef. Robert is a chef.
Now listen and write down the names of the towns where Guy and Robert live.
Like Roy, Guy lives in London. Guy lives in London.

Robert lives with Sue in New York. Robert lives with Sue in New York.

*Give candidates 30 seconds and then read each instruction **once** only.*

(Wait 10 seconds before going on to PART 4.)

PART FOUR, PART FOUR. *(Check that candidates have found PART 4.)*

Imagine a friend phones you to make arrangements for the two of you to meet and spend the day together tomorrow. Listen to what your friend says and make notes about where and when to meet and what to take with you. *(15 seconds)* Listen and make notes.

You will hear the information **twice**. Ready?

I'm really looking forward to our day at the beach tomorrow. Let's meet at the railway station. It's quite close to your house. Our train leaves at ten so if we meet at quarter to ten that should be OK. Don't forget to bring something to eat with you - we'll have a picnic on the beach. And remember your swimming things too, of course. I haven't swum for ages. It should be marvellous. And could you also bring that book you said you'd lend me? So that's three things to remember - something to eat, swimming things and book. See you at quarter to ten tomorrow.

(Wait 30 seconds before the second reading.)

Now listen again. Ready? *(Read the instructions again.)*

(60 seconds)

You now have 1 hour 40 minutes to complete the rest of the paper.

Practice Test Two

LISTENING TEST, PART ONE, PART ONE. *(Allow time to check that candidates have found PART 1.)*

In this first part you will hear five sentences. Match each sentence with one of those written on your answer sheet. First look at the example. If you hear: 'The population is one hundred thousand, one hundred thousand' the matching answer is C. Put a circle round your answer.

Now listen. I will read the important part of each sentence **twice.**

Number one, number one. *(6 seconds)*
  There are ninety-four thousand books in the library.
  There are ninety-four thousand books in the library.
(10 seconds)

Number two, number two. *(6 seconds)*
  They live in Gloucester. That's G-L-O-U-C-E-S-T-E-R, G-L-O-U-C-E-S-T-E-R.

(10 seconds)

Number three, number three. *(6 seconds)*
  The cinema is opposite the disco.
  The cinema is opposite the disco. *(10 seconds)*

Number four, number four. *(6 seconds)*
  My phone number is two-six-three-oh-one, two-six-three-oh-one. *(10 seconds)*

Number five, number five. *(6 seconds)*
  They got married in nineteen eighty-five.
  They got married in nineteen eighty-five. *(10 seconds)*

PART TWO, PART TWO. *(Check that candidates have found PART 2.)*

I'm going to read five sentences. Choose the best reply for each. Look at the example. If you hear: 'What time is it? What time is it?' the best answer is C. Put a circle round your answer.

Listen.
Number one, number one. *(6 seconds)*
  What do you do?
  What do you do? *(10 seconds)*

Number two, number two. *(6 seconds)*
  When's your birthday?
  When's your birthday? *(10 seconds)*

Number three, number three. *(6 seconds)*
  Let's have an ice cream.
  Let's have an ice cream. *(10 seconds)*

Number four, number four. *(6 seconds)*
  What are you doing this summer?
  What are you doing this summer? *(10 seconds)*

Number five, number five. *(6 seconds)*
  Is this seat free?
  Is this seat free? *(10 seconds)*

PART THREE, PART THREE. *(Check that candidates have found PART 3.)*

You are going to fill in a diary. Look at the diary now. *(15 seconds for looking at the page.)* Listen to the instructions. The words below the diary will help you. You will hear the information **twice**.

Ready? *(Allow 10 seconds between each instruction.)*

Opposite Tuesday the fourth of May write three p.m. Dentist. Opposite Tuesday the fourth of May write three p.m. Dentist.
Opposite Thursday the sixth of May write twelve thirty Lunch with John. Opposite Thursday the sixth of May write twelve thirty Lunch with John.
Opposite Friday the seventh of June write seven forty-five Theatre. Opposite Friday the seventh of June write seven forty-five Theatre.
Opposite Saturday the eighth of May write Party, 44 Main Street, eight thirty. Opposite Saturday the eighth of May write Party, 44 Main Street, eight thirty.

Give candidates 30 seconds and then read each instruction once only.

(Wait 10 seconds before going on to PART 4.)

PART FOUR, PART FOUR. *(Check that candidates have found PART 4.)*

You are going to fill in some information about a journey. Look at the form. *(15 seconds)* Listen and fill in the form.

You will hear the information **twice**. Ready?

Yes, I think I've got all the information about your flight here. The flight leaves from Gatwick, that's spelt G-A-T-W-I-C-K, on Friday the fourteenth of June. No sorry, not June, July, how stupid of me, Friday the fourteenth of July. It leaves at ten in the morning, so don't forget to get there by nine to have time to check in. It's flight number NZ 236 going to Auckland, that's A-U-C-K-L-A-N-D. I think you change at New York and Los Angeles. No, you only need to change at Los Angeles. You arrive in Auckland at ten thirty in the morning on Sunday the sixteenth of July local time. What a long flight! You'd better take plenty to read. Have a good trip!

(Wait 30 seconds before the second reading.)

Now listen again. Ready? *(Read the instructions again.)*

(60 seconds)

You now have 1 hour 40 minutes to complete the rest of the paper.

Practice Test Three

LISTENING TEST, PART ONE, PART ONE. *(Allow time to check that candidates have found PART 1.)*

In this first part you will hear five sentences. Match each sentence with one of those written on your answer sheet. First look at the example. If you hear: 'The population is one hundred thousand, one hundred thousand' the matching answer is C. Put a circle round your answer.

Now listen. I will read the important part of each sentence **twice**.

Number one, number one. *(6 seconds)*
There are seven hundred and sixty thousand owners of fish in Britain.
There are seven hundred and sixty thousand owners of fish in Britain *(10 seconds)*

Number two, number two. *(6 seconds)*
There are three books on the table.
There are three books on the table. *(10 seconds)*

Number three, number three. *(6 seconds)*
Ring me on five-double-four, nine-double-eight-three.
Ring me on five-double-four, nine-double-eight-three. *(10 seconds)*

Number four, number four. *(6 seconds)*
She comes from Leongatha, that's spelt L-E-O-N-G-A-T-H-A, that's L-E-O-N-G-A-T-H-A. *(10 seconds)*

Number five, number five. *(6 seconds)*
There's a large square with a small triangle in each of the two corners on the left-hand side and a small circle in each of the two right-hand corners.
There's a large square with a small triangle in each of the two corners on the left-hand side and a small circle in each of the two right-hand corners. *(10 seconds)*

PART TWO, PART TWO. *(Check that candidates have found PART 2.)*

I'm going to read five sentences. Choose the best reply for each. Look at the example. If you hear: 'What time is it? What time is it?' the best answer is C. Put a circle round your answer.

Listen.

Number one, number one. *(6 seconds)*
  What's fifteen minus eight?
  What's fifteen minus eight? *(10 seconds)*

Number two, number two. *(6 seconds)*
  How did you come here?
  How did you come here? *(10 seconds)*

Number three, number three. *(6 seconds)*
  Do you take milk in coffee?
  Do you take milk in coffee? *(10 seconds)*

Number four, number four. *(6 seconds)*
  How do you feel today?
  How do you feel today? *(10 seconds)*

Number five, number five. *(6 seconds)*
  Is Jane at home?
  Is Jane at home? *(10 seconds)*

PART THREE, PART THREE. *(Check that candidates have found PART 3.)*

You are going to complete a table. Look at the map showing a tour of Scotland. *(15 seconds for looking at the page.)* Listen and follow the instructions. You will hear the information **twice**. Ready? *(Allow 10 seconds between each instruction.)*

Write Perth on the table on the line under St Andrews. Write one night beside Perth.
Under Perth write Aberdeen. Write three nights beside Aberdeen. Under Perth write Aberdeen. Write three nights beside Aberdeen.
Under Aberdeen write Inverness. Write four nights beside Inverness. Under Aberdeen write Inverness. Write four nights beside Inverness.
Write Ullapool under Inverness. Write two nights beside Ullapool. Write Ullapool under Inverness. Write two nights beside Ullapool.

Under Ullapool write Oban. Beside Oban write three nights. Under Ullapool write Oban. Beside Oban write three nights.
On the bottom line write Edinburgh. Write one night beside Edinburgh on the bottom line. On the bottom line write Edinburgh. Write one night beside Edinburgh on the bottom line.

Give candidates 30 seconds and then read each instruction once only.

(Wait 10 seconds before going on to PART 4.)

PART FOUR, PART FOUR. *(Check that candidates have found PART 4.)*

Imagine you are going to stay in a friend's home while your friend is on holiday. Your friend telephones you and gives you some instructions about what to do while you are there. Make a note of the instructions which your friend gives you. *(15 seconds)*

You will hear the information **twice**. Ready?

I hope you'll enjoy yourself at my place. Do make yourself at home. I wonder if you'd mind doing a couple of things for me while you're there. First if any letters come for me could you post them on to me. I'll be staying at the Ritz Hotel, that's R-I-T-Z, 21 North Street, Rye, that's R-Y-E. Thanks a lot. I'm expecting one or two quite important letters. The other thing is would you mind feeding the cat. She needs a tin of food and a bit of milk every day. You'll find the tins of cat food in the kitchen cupboard. Finally, if you have any problems ring my sister. You know Anne, don't you? Her number is two-six-one-oh-five. No, sorry, I've made a mistake, it's two-six-one-oh-four. I always get confused with her number for some reason. That's two-six-one-oh-four. Have a lovely time. See you next month.

(Wait 30 seconds before the second reading.)

Now listen again. Ready? *(Read the instructions again.)*

(60 seconds)

You now have 1 hour 40 minutes to complete the rest of the paper.

Practice Test Four

LISTENING TEST, PART ONE, PART ONE. (Allow time to check that candidates have found PART 1.)

In this first part you will hear five sentences. Match each sentence with one of those written on your answer sheet. First look at the example. If you hear: 'The population is one hundred thousand, one hundred thousand' the matching answer is C. Put a circle round your answer.

Now listen. I will read the important part of each sentence **twice**.

Number one, number one. *(6 seconds)*
   I'm living in Aldeburgh, that's A-L-D-E-B-U-R-G-H, that's A-L-D-E-B-U-R-G-H.
   (10 seconds)

Number two, number two. *(6 seconds)*
   His number is six-five-eight, three-seven-one.
   His number is six-five-eight, three-seven-one.
(10 seconds)

Number three, number three. *(6 seconds)*
   The shoe shop is between the newsagent's and the grocer's.
   The shoe shop is between the newsagent's and the grocer's. *(10 seconds)*

Number four, number four. *(6 seconds)*
   The college was founded in seventeen forty-two, in seventeen forty-two.
   (10 seconds)

Number five, number five. *(6 seconds)*
   The party is on the thirtieth of June.
   The party is on the thirtieth of June. *(10 seconds)*

PART TWO, PART TWO. *(Check that candidates have found PART 2.)*

I'm going to read five sentences. Choose the best reply for each. Look at the example. If you hear: 'What time is it? What time is it?' the best answer is C. Put a circle round your answer.

Listen.

Number one, number one. *(6 seconds)*
   Would you like a biscuit?
   Would you like a biscuit? *(10 seconds)*

Number two, number two. *(6 seconds)*
   What's your job?
   What's your job? *(10 seconds)*

Number three, number three. *(6 seconds)*
   What's thirty-one plus two?
   What's thirty-one plus two? *(10 seconds)*

Number four, number four. *(6 seconds)*
   What's Fred like?
   What's Fred like? *(10 seconds)*

Number five, number five. *(6 seconds)*
   Can I help you?
   Can I help you? *(10 seconds)*

PART THREE, PART THREE. *(Check that candidates have found PART 3.)*

You are going to complete a chart. Look at the chart. It gives some information about hotels you are thinking of staying in. *(15 seconds for looking at the page.)* Listen to the instructions and complete the chart. You will hear the information **twice**. Ready? *(Allow 10 seconds between each instruction.)*

Listen and write in the following extra information about the Star Hotel.
The Star Hotel is not near the station. It is not near the station.
The telephone number of the Star Hotel is four-five-one, two-double-oh-seven, four-five-one, two-double-oh-seven.
Now listen and write in the following extra information about the Luxe Hotel.
The Luxe Hotel costs forty pounds a night. The Luxe Hotel costs forty pounds a night.
There is a phone in every room. There is a phone in every room.
Every room also has a shower. Every room has a shower.

You take bus number thirty-eight to get to the city
centre, that's bus number thirty-eight.
Now listen and write in the following extra information
about the George Hotel.
The George Hotel doesn't have a phone in every room.
The George Hotel doesn't have a phone in every room.
There is also not a shower in every room. There is also
not a shower in every room.
It is near the station. It is near the station.
The phone number of the George Hotel is seven-one-
nine, six-eight-four-oh, seven-one-nine, six-eight-four-
oh.

Give candidates 30 seconds and then read each instruction
once *only.*

(Wait 10 seconds before going on to PART 4.)

PART FOUR, PART FOUR. *(Check that candidates
have found PART 4.)*

Imagine that one of your grandparents phones you and
asks you to do some shopping for them. Listen to the
message and make a list of what you have to buy. *(15
seconds)* Listen and make a list.

You will hear the information **twice**.   Ready?

I'd be so grateful if you could possibly do some shopping
for us when you're in town. I don't feel too well today and
I'd like to stay at home but there are one or two things we
badly need. First of all, some fruit. Could you get us some
oranges - about six, please. Perhaps some apples? No,
we've still got some apples. Some bananas then, about
half a dozen of them too, please. And a cucumber too if
they've got a nice one. If it's not too much trouble, could
you also get us a newspaper, a copy of *The Times*, please.
And finally, I think we need some matches, a box of
matches. Oh, no, Phil's just found some. But we do
definitely need a bottle of milk. Hope all this won't be too
much to carry. Thank you so much. See you later.

(Wait 30 seconds before the second reading.)

Now listen again. Ready? *(Read the instructions again.)*

(60 seconds)

You now have 1 hour 40 minutes to complete the rest of
the paper.

Answers to Practice Tests

Practice Test One

Listening

Part 1	Part 2
1 D	1 B
2 A	2 A
3 C	3 B
4 B	4 C
5 B	5 A

Part 3

The Naunton Family

Name	Age	Job	Where he or she lives
Roy	<u>30</u>	Policeman	London
Guy	28	<u>Dentist</u>	<u>London</u>
Leo	<u>26</u>	<u>Zookeeper</u>	Bristol
Robert	<u>25</u>	<u>Chef</u>	<u>New York</u>
Sue	<u>23</u>	<u>Scientist</u>	New York

Part 4

Meet at the railway station at 9.45. Bring something to eat, swimming things and book.

English Usage

1	it	6	asked	11	too
2	had	7	answered	12	some
3	because	8	have	13	where
4	a	9	cold	14	up
5	with	10	by	15	away

Reading One

1 B; 2 D; 3 D; 4 D; 5 B.

Reading Two

The postcards should be labelled in the following order: Top row, left to right: Aunt Flo, Ricky, Sandra, Uncle Jim. Bottom row, left to right: Louise, Helen, Tom, Chris.

Reading Three

Balmoral; 100 years old; 200 metres; yes; 30; 15; 30; Quantock Hills, Somerset beaches; 0643 2288.

Reading and Writing

James Stewart
13 Glasgow Drive
Edinburgh
Scotland
ED1 4XC

Dear James,

I'm fine and my sister is much better now. I'm coming to Scotland on the 11th April and can stay for a week. My train arrives at ten fifteen on Saturday 11th in the morning. It'd be great if you'd meet me. I'd love to go to the mountains for a few days.

With best wishes,

(Student's own name)

Writing

No model answers are given for this or for any other of the Writing questions in the Practice Tests. For an idea of the length and the complexity of the compositions expected of the best students at this level, see the model compositions provided at the end of the Elementary Exam Help section.

Practice Test Two

Listening

Part 1	Part 2
1 C	1 C
2 B	2 D
3 B	3 A
4 D	4 D
5 A	5 C

Part 3
Add to diary:
(Tuesday) 3 p.m. Dentist; (Thursday) 12.30 Lunch with John; (Friday) 7.45 Theatre; (Saturday) Party 44 Main Street, 8.30.

Part 4
Friday 14th July, 10 a.m.; Gatwick; NZ 236; Auckland; Los Angeles; 10.30 a.m. Sunday 16th July.

English Usage

1	from	6	an	11	further
2	takes	7	at	12	back
3	there	8	had	13	was
4	spend	9	until	14	last
5	because	10	told	15	time

Reading One

1 B; 2 A; 3 C; 4 D; 5 B.

Reading Two

The children from left to right are Diana, Paul, John, Peter, Tina, Sally.

Reading Three

Newtown; Green Lane; 1,000; 350; 116; John Barnes; January 1994; food, children's clothes, newspapers, magazines and cosmetics.

Reading and Writing

Get off the bus at the stop on Mill Road. Turn left and walk along Mill Road until you come to Central Park. Turn left just before the park. Take the second turning on the right. That is Castle Street. I live at number 41. It's on the right-hand side of the road. You can't miss it.

Writing

No model answers are given for this or for any other of the Writing questions in the Practice Tests. For an idea of the length and the complexity of the compositions expected of the best students at this level, see the model compositions provided at the end of the Elementary Exam Help section.

Practice Test Three

Listening

Part 1		Part 2	
1	B	1	B
2	D	2	C
3	D	3	A
4	A	4	B
5	D	5	C

Part 3

Perth 1 night; Aberdeen 3 nights; Inverness 4 nights; Ullapool 2 nights; Oban 3 nights; Edinburgh 1 night.

Part 4

Post letters on to Ritz Hotel, 21 North Street, Rye.
Feed cat - tin of food (in cupboard) and some milk every day.
If problems, ring sister, Anna, 26104.

English Usage

1	were	6	to	11	said
2	of	7	own	12	on
3	there	8	better	13	had
4	Then	9	no	14	told
5	in	10	not	15	anyone

Reading One

1 B; 2 D; 3 C; 4 A; 5 D.

Reading Two

M should go in the box just above the railway line on the left-hand side of the page and the route to it is the obvious one leaving town on the A33 and turning left and then third right.
Z should go in the box in the top right-hand corner. The route there is along the A33 and then takes the third turning on the right.

Reading Three

Joseph likes tennis and swimming but he doesn't like skiing or riding.
Daniel likes tennis, skiing and riding but he doesn't like swimming.
Mary likes tennis, swimming and riding but she doesn't like skiing.
Anna likes tennis and swimming but she doesn't like skiing or riding.

Reading and Writing

Sue is quite tall and slim. She has long dark hair and wears glasses. She is wearing jeans, a shirt, a denim jacket, a scarf and boots. She is carrying a shoulder bag and an umbrella. She has two suitcases with her, a small one and a large one. Her suitcases have a stripe round the bottom.

Writing

No model answers are given for this or for any other of the Writing questions in the Practice Tests. For an idea of the length and the complexity of the compositions expected of the best students at this level, see the model compositions provided at the end of the Elementary Exam Help section.

Listening

Part 1

1 B
2 C
3 C
4 D
5 B

Part 2

1 A
2 D
3 B
4 B
5 C

Part 3

	Star Hotel	Luxe Hotel	George Hotel
Price per night	£30	£40	£25
Phone in room?	No	Yes	No
Shower in room?	Yes	Yes	No
Near station?	No	No	Yes
Bus to city centre?	Bus no. 21	Bus no. 38	Bus no. 45
Tel. no.	451 2007	634 2241	719 6840

Part 4

6 oranges; 6 bananas; a cucumber; *The Times*; a bottle of milk.

English Usage

1 which
2 because
3 is
4 few
5 quite
6 and
7 without
8 after
9 lying
10 No-one
11 for
12 something
13 found
14 old
15 a

Reading One

1 D; 2 A; 3 B; 4 A; 5 D.

Reading Two

From left to right – at the far side of the table – Grandfather, Sonia and – at the ends and near side of the table – Mrs Smith, Billy, Dick, Grandmother, Mr Smith.

Reading Three

From left to right – on the church side of the road – church, cafe, bank, post office, cinema and – on the other side of the road – chemist's, school, bookshop, swimming pool.

Reading and Writing

Thanks for your letter. I'd love to see the new Dustin Hoffmann film but I'm afraid I'm very busy next week. On Monday evening I'm playing tennis with Anna. On Tuesday I have my evening class. On Wednesday I'm having dinner at Aunt Jean's and on Thursday I'm going to the theatre with Jane and Bill. I'm free on Friday evening but on Saturday I'm going to a party. Would you be free to go to see the film on Friday?

Writing

No model answers are given for this or for any other of the Writing questions in the Practice Tests. For an idea of the length and the complexity of the compositions expected of the best students at this level, see the model compositions provided at the end of the Elementary Exam Help section.

Pitman ESOL Practice Tests – Intermediate Level

Exam Help

Listening

p.7 ex. 1

There are many different ways of answering some of these questions. Here are some suggestions below.

a Anyone who wanted to know the time could be asking this, though note that it is quite an informal version of 'What time is it?' A good answer would be 'Six o'clock'.

b Two people at a party perhaps, discussing someone else at the other side of the room. 'She's a secretary'.

c Anyone indoors feeling rather cold. 'Shall I close the window?'

d Someone offering you a cup of tea or coffee. 'Yes, one spoonful, please.'

e A waiter in a restaurant. 'Yes, I'll have the steak, please.'

f Someone offering help, for example to someone with a lot of luggage. 'No, I can manage, thanks.'

g Someone answering the phone at the switchboard of a company called Brooks Brothers. 'Can I speak to the manager, please?'

h Someone on the telephone when the person who has been rung up is not available. 'No, it's all right. I'll ring back later.'

i A teacher, perhaps, in the middle of a long lesson, feeling that the students need a rest. 'When shall we come back?'

j Two friends talking about another friend. 'Yes, she passed with flying colours.'

k A mother to her son perhaps. She finds the television or the music too loud. 'Oh, all right.'

l Two friends talking about another friend. 'Oh dear, what's the matter?'

m Someone who thinks their friend looks upset. 'I've just lost my job.'

n Someone with a car arranging to give someone else a lift. 'OK, I'll be ready and waiting.'

o Two friends at a party and one of them wants to leave. 'Yes, I suppose so or we'll miss the last bus.'

p Two people out shopping together and one feels the other might be thirsty. 'Yes, let's go into that cafe on the corner.'

q Two strangers on a train and one is feeling rather hot. 'Not at all.'

r Two strangers in a cafe. 'No, it's free.'

s Someone at the switchboard of a company when the extension that the person calling wishes to speak to is engaged. 'No, I'll call back later.'

t Two friends puzzled by some strange situation. 'I really don't know what to think.'

u One friend surprised by the other's appearance. 'I've been painting the ceiling.'

v Two friends who haven't seen each other for ages. 'Yes, what have you been doing with yourself?'

w Two friends meeting in the street. 'I'm going to the park. Do you feel like coming?'

x A friend talking to someone whose birthday it is. 'Thanks.'

y A son apologising to his mother. 'Never mind. It can wait until tomorrow.'

z Someone who's just got a driving licence, perhaps. 'Congratulations.'

p 8 ex. 2

Answers

A g; B l; C o; D i; E b; F e; G j; H c; I n; J f; K h; L m; M a; N d; O k; P p.

pp. 9-10 ex. 5

Text to read to the students.

a She's quite an interesting character and I hope you'll meet her while you're in Scotland. Her name's Rhoda, that's spelt R-H-O-D-A, and her surname's Blair, that's B-L-A-I-R, I think. Let me check. No, it's actually got an E on the end, B-L-A-I-R-E. She lives with her husband, Dan, on the Isle of Eigg, and you don't spell that quite like the egg in omelette even though it's pronounced the same way. There's an I after the E. Their address is very simple. It's just Sea House, Main Street, Eigg. If you get to the island anyone will be able to help you to find them. Rhoda is a teacher in the only school on the island – we met when we were doing our teacher training course together. She's got three children and they all go to her school. I imagine they make up quite a proportion of her pupils there. Their two oldest children are boys – Alexander and Bill – and the youngest is a girl, Mhairi. That's pronounced 'Vahri' but is spelt M-H-A-I-R-I. There's two years between each of the children and Alexander, the oldest, must be eight now. No, he was born two years after Rhoda and I were at college so he's ten already and Bill's eight. How time flies! Rhoda was always very fond of swimming and she'll be able to show you the best places to swim on the island – you'll be surprised how warm the sea can be there. Do try and persuade her to play her guitar for you too. She's really good at it and her singing voice is lovely too. In fact, her ambition is to make a record of traditional Scottish folk songs. She'd play the guitar and she and her husband and children would sing. I hope she'll find an interested company one day.

b I'd be really grateful if you could do a few jobs for me while you're in town. I find it so hard to get into the city centre these days with my bad leg and yet there are some things I really need to get done. First of all, I've got a film waiting to be collected at the chemist's on the Market Square. Could you get it for me, please. The reference number is ER 338 and it's twenty colour prints. I'm sure they'll be ready. My neighbour took them in a week ago and they said they'd probably only take three days. That's the first thing. The second is could you please get me a card for my neighbour who's just had a baby. Something suitable for a new baby boy, please. I can't find anything appropriate in our local shops here. Then I'd also like some wool to make the baby a hat. 250 grammes of white wool should be enough. Get good quality and really soft wool as it's for a baby. It doesn't matter if it's very expensive. I could also do with a new pair of knitting needles. Ask for size 9. Don't get any other size if they haven't got nines in. The last thing is, I wonder if you could possibly buy me a box of Swiss chocolates. They don't sell them near here and I'd like them for your grandfather's birthday. You know how he loves them. Spend about ten pounds. OK? Hope all this is clear. Ring me back if you can't manage to do any of these things and again I do apologise for troubling you.

c We run a number of different photography courses. In fact there's one almost every day. They are all taught by Jane Fisher who is a successful professional photographer. Miss Fisher does three day-time courses – one on Monday, one on Tuesday and one on Saturday. Those all start at ten a.m. and finish at twelve. On Wednesdays and Thursdays she also does an evening class starting at 7.30. That finishes at nine p.m. The Monday and Wednesday classes are in advanced photography. The others are really suitable for everyone regardless of their level of experience. All Miss Fisher's courses take place in room 2B, which is a spacious studio on the second floor. The day-time courses last for a whole year but the evening ones are for three months only, although many students choose to come back for a succession of courses. It costs £60 for a year's course and only £20 for a three-month course. That includes the use of all the facilities at the Community Centre. Cookery classes are special in that they even run on Sundays. Mr Chowdhury, C-H-O-W-D-H-U-R-Y, does a course in Indian cuisine on Sunday afternoons from 2 to 4. That's a very popular course so book early. It lasts for ten weeks, takes place in the college kitchens and costs only £30. That's £30 for the ten-week course and you take home lots of delicious food which you have prepared for your families under Mr Chowdhury's guidance. There is also a range of morning cookery courses. These vary from month to month and you should contact the College Secretary to check what is happening this month. Special mention can be made now, however, of the Tuesday evening course in traditional English cookery. Your teacher here is the well-known local cook and proprietor of one of our town's most popular restaurants, Mrs Anne Matthews. Her traditional English cookery course lasts three months and costs only £25. Mrs Matthews also runs another evening course on Thursday evenings. This one specialises in party cooking. Both of Mrs Matthews' courses also take place in the college kitchens and each class lasts 2 hours starting at 7.30. The party cookery course is rather cheaper than the traditional English one at only £22. Book early for all these cookery courses as numbers are limited and both Mr Chowdhury and Mrs Matthews are very popular teachers.

Answers

a

Name	Rhoda Blaire
Address	Sea House, Main Street, Eigg
Job	teacher

Children's names and ages Alexander (10), Bill (8) and Mhairi (6)

Hobbies	swimming, guitar playing and singing
Ambitions	make a record of traditional Scottish folk songs.

b collect film from chemist's, Market Sq, ER 338 (20 colour prints); get card for new baby boy; buy 250 gr. soft white wool, good quality; get pair no. 9 knitting needles; buy box of Swiss chocolates (spend about £10).

c Photography courses – Sat. 10-12, Wed. and Thurs. 7.30–9; taught by Miss Fisher in 2B, Sat. course for a year but other two for 3 months, £60 for year and £20 for 3 months.

Cookery courses – Sun. 2–4, taught by Mr Chowdhury (Indian cuisine), held in college kitchens, last 10 weeks, £30. Also Tues. and Thurs. evenings, 7.30–9.30, taught by Mrs Anne Matthews, Tues. course in traditional English cooking, £25. Thurs. one in party cooking, college kitchens, £22.

English Usage

p. 12 ex. 1
Answers

a elephants; b two; c picking grasses, etc., lifting heavy things, stroking; d teeth which continue growing throughout life; e for their valuable tusks.

p. 12 ex. 2
Answers

1 (auxiliary or modal) verb or adverb; 2 a number; 3 pronoun; 4 adjective (comparative); 5 preposition; 6 verb (gerund); 7 (possessive) adjective; 8 (relative) pronoun; 9 article; 10 (auxiliary) verb; 11 noun; 12 verb (infinitive).

p. 12 ex. 4
Answers

1 can; 2 two; 3 it; 4 larger; 5 for; 6 lifting; 7 its; 8 which; 9 a; 10 have; 11 elephants; 12 be.

p. 13
Answers

1 at; 2 was; 3 it; 4 mouth; 5 has; 6 city; 7 with; 8 but; 9 to; 10 visiting; 11 as; 12 must; 13 its;

14 can; 15 once; 16 times; 17 usually; 18 the; 19 particularly; 20 playing.

Reading One

pp.14-15 ex. 1
Answers

a he was full of excited anticipation ; b But the old ones are gold; c *to concentrate on* or *to consist of;* d it has very rich educational and cultural traditions; e would you perhaps like to get some extra qualifications.

p. 15 ex. 2
Answers

a A is wrong because it is clear from the context that only a sentence saying something negative about society could fit; B follows on from the preceding sentence in a reasonably logical way but does not make a logical connection with the following sentence; C is, like A, too positive in tone. D is correct.

b A is wrong because it suddenly mentions 'He' which makes no logical sense here; B is far too long to fit the form of the verse; the 'it' in C logically could refer only to 'drop' in the preceding line but 'drop' is too small to say 'You'd have drunk it all up' about. D fits the meaning and the form of the verse.

c A would follow logically on from 'in other words' rather than from 'for example'; B lists a lot of vegetables as well as fruits; C might have fitted in after the first or second sentence, perhaps, but it cannot follow 'for example'; D is correct.

d A almost fits and would be all right if the next sentence said 'would be' rather than 'would have been'; B is not a complete sentence and the punctuation makes it clear that a complete sentence is required; C fits well with the preceding sentence but not with the one which follows; D fits from every point of view.

e A is far too frank for an advertisement; B might be all right (if not altogether natural) if the tense were 'it will be' rather than 'it's'; C an imperative rather than a gerund is required – if 'see' were substituted for 'seeing' then this alternative would be satisfactory; D fits from both the meaning and the grammar point of view.

f A is appropriate for an advert, perhaps, but not for a formal letter of this type; B is not appropriate for this kind of letter where it is clear that the original letter is only an initial enquiry rather than an application; C is far too informal for this sort of formal letter; D fits in terms of both meaning and register.

Reading Two

p. 17 ex. 1

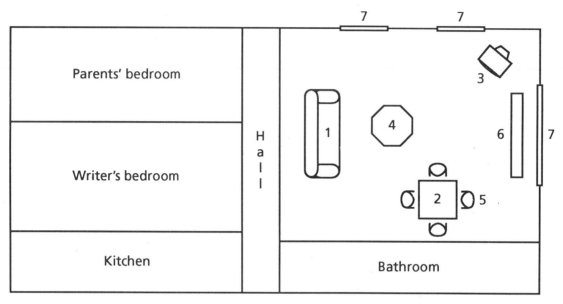

1 sofa,   2 table,   3 TV,   4 table,   5 chairs,   6 bookcase,   7 windows

p. 18 ex. 4

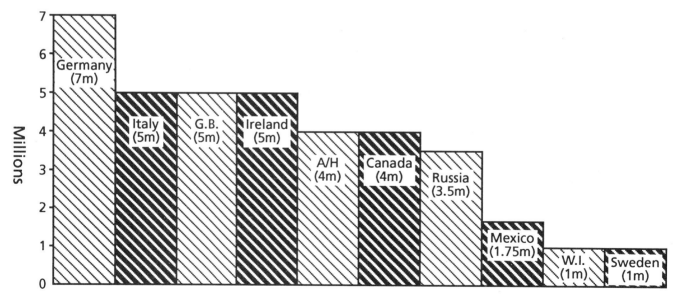

Countries of origin of immigrants to the USA, 1820 - 1987

Reading Three

p. 19
1 4; 2 romantic; 3 7.30; 4 Dracula 1992; 5 Twentieth Century Robin Hood; 6 Arts Cinema; 7 Mark Manly; 8 Jumbo 3.

Reading and Writing

p.20 ex. 1
The points in the letter which are relevant to your answer are:

> three months off before college
> need to earn money
> want to travel
> combine work with travel
> no qualifications
> experience with small children
> don't mind hard work
> want to be with other people
> parents not too keen – unless, perhaps, something connected with studies
> any bright ideas?

The reply could, therefore, suggest something involving work with children – nannying, children's camps – or it could involve something requiring no qualifications – hotel work, fruit picking, for example. There must be some connection made with studies – perhaps the point could be made that the person's knowledge of languages will improve.

p. 21 ex. 2
1 House number and street; 2 Day and month; 3 Dear; 4 Thank; 5 for; 6 to; 7 tell; 8 to; 9 be; 10 love; 11 since; 12 time; 13 catch; 14 hearing; 15 love (best wishes); 16 first name.

p. 21 ex. 3
a things; b well; c but; d great / lovely / wonderful / good / nice; e regards / best wishes / love; f Remember; g seeing; h hear; i write; j touch; k very.

Writing

pp. 22-3 ex. 3
a swam; b Have you ever dived ...; c had learnt; d swimming; e was approaching; f were; g has fallen, is helping.

p. 23 ex. 4
a at; b at; c on; d in; e in; f in; g of; h for; i of.

p. 24 ex. 5
The corrections that need to be made are:
... I have been to the swimming pool at least twice a week ....if you want to learn .... some water-wings... quite young ....even teach their six-month .....get used to being ... keep your balance in the water ....you will quickly start making good progress ... After that, you can learn ....interested in ....I love ... gracefully ....anyone at any age.

Model Compositions

p.24 ex. 7
Of course, there are many different ways of writing the compositions set. Students may well write better ones than those presented below. However, the compositions below are given as examples of work of the length and kind of complexity expected of better students at Pitman Intermediate level.

a My favourite sport and how to do it
My favourite sport is swimming. I started to learn when I was about seven years old. When I was younger I used to go swimming three or four times a week. Now I have less free time but a week never goes by without my visiting the pool at least once.

Swimming is an inexpensive and simple sport. You do not need any complicated equipment. You just need a swimming costume or trunks and perhaps a cap. You can swim in the sea or a river or you can go to a special swimming pool.

The first thing you need to learn when swimming is how to float in the water. You can help yourself do this by wearing a ring or by putting water wings on your arms. As soon as you can float, you are ready to learn some basic swimming strokes like breast-stroke, backstroke and crawl.

A big step forward in swimming is when you learn to dive. This is a way of jumping into the water arms and head – rather than feet – first. It is hard at first but diving smoothly into the water is a marvellous feeling.

I love swimming because it is very good exercise for

my whole body. Last but not least, I would recommend it because it is so convenient to do: you can do it when you like and for as long as you like.

b The main problems for young people in my country at the moment

There is one main problem above all others for young people in my country at the moment and that is unemployment.

In some areas there is only a fifteen per cent chance of school-leavers finding a job. In other areas the problem is not quite so acute but there is no part of the country where a school-leaver without any further education can be sure of getting work. Even when young people do attend some further education courses and gain some qualifications, they are still not guaranteed work. There are even quite large numbers of unemployed university graduates now.

This problem of unemployment brings other problems with it. Discipline in schools is bad as many pupils do not see any point in working hard at school now. Young people need and want money. If they cannot earn it, some of them turn to crime. No longer able to find excitement and a sense of purpose through work, some young people are tempted to try drugs. Worst of all perhaps, is the feeling of hopelessness which many young people have.

In my opinion, it is high time that the government did something to solve the problem of unemployment. I believe that when unemployment ceases to be a problem for young people, then problems of school discipline, juvenile crime and drugs will dramatically decline.

c '...What is the food like in your country and could you give me a typical recipe?' Write a letter in reply to a penfriend who asks you this question.

Dear Anne,

Thank you very much for your letter. It was interesting to hear all your news. I hope your sister is feeling better now.

You ask about typical food in my country. Food in my country is determined by the fact that the land in my country is quite poor. Not much grows there. The main staple crop is oats and much of the land is given over to the grazing of sheep. So we eat a lot of lamb and we have a lot of food which uses oats in different ways –

porridge for breakfast, oatcakes instead of bread and oatmeal puddings instead of potatoes.

However, the food in my country is made more varied by the fact that we also have lots of fish and plenty of game. Fishing and hunting are important in my country. We have, for example, wonderful locally produced salmon and shellfish as well as venison and various game birds.

Here is a very simple but very delicious recipe from Scotland. Take some herring – Scottish if at all possible. Coat them in egg and then in fine oatmeal. Then fry them gently in butter. Serve with lemon. They are wonderful.

The best way for you to learn about our food is to come and visit us and to try it for yourself. Why don't you come some time next year?

With all good wishes,
   Felicity

d The most exciting experience I have ever had

The most exciting experience I have ever had was the day when I witnessed the finding of hidden treasure.

It was my twelfth birthday and I was on holiday with my parents in the Shetland Islands in the far north of Scotland. My father was in charge of an archaeological dig there. He and his students were excavating the ruins of an old church. My mother was kept busy cooking for all the hungry diggers and I was having a wonderful time exploring the island, swimming and playing on the beaches.

On my birthday I decided for once to help a little with the digging. I was scraping away at the soft earth beside ten or twelve others. Suddenly the person beside me called out 'What do you think this is?' He had hit something green and hard. My father came running. Soon everyone was gathered round and some green bowls and then some brooches were slowly and carefully brought out of the ground.

It took a long time and I was getting a bit impatient. I wanted everyone to come and eat my birthday cake. But people were too excited to think about food. Eventually there was quite a pile of objects on the ground.

It turned out that they were made of silver and had probably been hidden in the church when the Vikings invaded the Shetlands in the eleventh century. They had not seen the light of day for nine hundred years!

Listening Scripts

N.B. The text which is not in italics should be read aloud. It should be read at normal reading speed making it sound as much like spoken English (as opposed to English read aloud) as possible.

Practice Test One

PART ONE, PART ONE. *(Allow time to check that candidates have found PART 1.)*

In this first part you will hear ten sentences. Each sentence will be said twice. Choose the best reply for each one. Look at the example. *(15 seconds.)*

If you hear: 'What's the matter? You look very pale', the best answer is C. Put a circle round your answers.

Listen.

Number one, number one. *(5 seconds)*
  Do you mind if I open the window?
  Do you mind if I open the window? *(6 seconds)*

Number two, number two. *(5 seconds)*
  Which train are you catching?
  Which train are you catching? *(6 seconds)*

Number three, number three. *(5 seconds)*
  My sister's just had a baby.
  My sister's just had a baby. *(6 seconds)*

Number four, number four. *(5 seconds)*
  Have you been to Canada?
  Have you been to Canada? *(6 seconds)*

Number five, number five. *(5 seconds)*
  She's on the other line. Will you hold?
  She's on the other line. Will you hold? *(6 seconds)*

Number six, number six. *(5 seconds)*
  I feel like an ice cream.
  I feel like an ice cream. *(6 seconds)*

Number seven, number seven. *(5 seconds)*
  Could you do me a favour?
  Could you do me a favour? *(6 seconds)*

Number eight, number eight. *(5 seconds)*
  Please don't forget to keep in touch.
  Please don't forget to keep in touch. *(6 seconds)*

Number nine, number nine. *(5 seconds)*
  Why don't we go to the cinema tonight?
  Why don't we go to the cinema tonight? *(6 seconds)*

Number ten, number ten. *(5 seconds)*
  I think we'd better order a taxi.
  I think we'd better order a taxi. *(6 seconds)*

PART TWO, PART TWO. *(Allow time to check that candidates have found PART 2.)*

Look at the pictures in your answer book. You are going to listen to some information about one kind of sign language in English. This is one way of talking with the hands which is used by some deaf people in Britain. This sign language has a different gesture for each letter of the alphabet. All the gestures illustrated on the page mean one letter of the alphabet. Look at the pictures now. *(30 seconds)*

Ready? Now listen to the information and write the letter which each picture signifies in the box beside that gesture.

(Read each of the following statements twice, waiting ten seconds between each statement.)

The letter X is represented by crossing the index fingers over each other to make a shape that looks like an X. You make the letter M by holding up one hand with the fingers outstretched and the palm facing outwards. You then place the three extended middle fingers of the other hand across the open palm.
The letter N is made in the same way as the letter M except that two fingers are used instead of three.
The letter A is made by touching the thumb of one hand with the index finger of the other hand.
The letter C is made by holding the thumb and index finger of one hand in such a way that they seem to form a letter C.

The letter H is like the sign for the letter M except that four fingers are placed over the palm of the other hand instead of three.

When you hold your two fists on top of each other with the fingers all curled up you make the letter G.

The letter U is made by pointing to the little finger of one hand with the index finger of the other hand.

An S is made by hooking the little finger of one hand over the little finger of the other hand.

You make a T by pointing to the side of one palm with the index finger of the other hand.

*(After reading wait for 30 seconds and then read the statements above again **once** only.)*

PART THREE, PART THREE.   *(Check that candidates have found PART 3.)*

Look at your answer book. You want to travel from London to Leningrad and have asked a friend to organise your tickets for you. Look at the form now. *(30 seconds)*

Ready? Listen to what your friend tells you and fill in the details of your journey on the form. You will hear the information **once** only.

I've managed to fix up your travel arrangements as you asked. You've got a flight on Finnair to Helsinki on Thursday July the sixth. The plane leaves London Heathrow at one thirty-five in the afternoon. The flight takes just over two and a half hours but Finland is two hours ahead of British time and so you don't get there until six fifteen local time. It'll take you about half an hour to get into the centre of Helsinki from the airport. I've booked you a room right in the centre of the city. It's beside both the air terminal and the railway station and so all your transfers should be very straightforward. The hotel is called the Vaakuna, that's V-A-A-K-U-N-A. It's very nice with a lovely roof restaurant - I stayed there myself a couple of years ago. You go on to Leningrad by train the next day. The train leaves at lunchtime, at one o'clock to be precise and gets into the Finland Station in Leningrad at eight forty. You'll be coming back a week later, on Friday July the fourteenth. Your train leaves Leningrad at ten thirty-five in the morning and gets into Helsinki at ten past

four. It isn't really quicker going west, it's just that there's another hour's time difference between Finland and Leningrad. You'll be at the Vaakuna again on the way back but you're staying there a bit longer this time. As you requested I've got you a flight a few days later so that you'll have some time to sightsee in Finland. Your flight back to London is on Tuesday the eighteenth at two o'clock in the afternoon and it gets into Heathrow at quarter to three!   Pretty quick, you'll agree.   If there are any problems with all of this ring the travel agent - their number is oh-seven-one, six-eight three, double-five-nine-six. Oh, I'd better give you your reference number in case you need to contact the travel agent - it's AGY seven–two–oh–three. Let me know if you want me to pick up your tickets when they are ready - it'll probably take a week or so.

(After reading wait 60 seconds.)

Stop writing please.

You now have 2 hours 10 minutes to complete the rest of the paper.

Practice Test Two

PART ONE, PART ONE.   *(Allow time to check that candidates have found PART 1.)*

In this first part you will hear ten sentences. Each sentence will be said **twice.** Choose the best reply for each one. Look at the example. *(15 seconds.)*

If you hear: 'What's the matter? You look very pale', the best answer is C. Put a circle round your answers.

Listen.

Number one, number one. *(5 seconds)*
    What was your journey like?
    What was your journey like? *(6 seconds)*

Number two, number two. *(5 seconds)*
    He's feeling a bit under the weather.
    He's feeling a bit under the weather. *(6 seconds)*

Number three, number three. *(5 seconds)*
    Julie Collins' phone. Can I help you?
    Julie Collins' phone. Can I help you? *(6 seconds)*

Number four, number four. *(5 seconds)*
   I've got an exam tomorrow.
   I've got an exam tomorrow. *(6 seconds)*

Number five, number five. *(5 seconds)*
   It's getting late. It's time we made a move.
   It's getting late. It's time we made a move. *(6 seconds)*

Number six, number six. *(5 seconds)*
   How long have you been here?
   How long have you been here? *(6 seconds)*

Number seven, number seven. *(5 seconds)*
   It looks like rain again.
   It looks like rain again. *(6 seconds)*

Number eight, number eight. *(5 seconds)*
   What do you fancy?
   What do you fancy? *(6 seconds)*

Number nine, number nine. *(5 seconds)*
   Could you see your way to lending me five pounds?
   Could you see your way to lending me five pounds? *(6 seconds)*

Number ten, number ten. *(5 seconds)*
   Well I never!
   Well I never! *(6 seconds)*

PART TWO, PART TWO. *(Allow time to check that candidates have found PART 2.)*

You want to sell a television and are going to draw an advertisement for it. Look at the picture of the television in your book. *(10 seconds)*

Ready? Now listen and follow the instructions.
*(Read each instruction **twice** leaving ten seconds between each instruction.)*

Above the picture of the television write in block capitals 'TV FOR SALE'.
Below the picture write in ordinary handwriting 'Only forty pounds'.
Put an exclamation mark after the price.
On the top left-hand side of the page draw three asterisks one below the other.
Beside the first asterisk write 'Only two years old' . Put

'only' in capitals but the rest in ordinary writing.
Beside the bottom asterisk write - in ordinary writing– 'In good condition'.
Underline 'In good condition'.
Beside the middle asterisk write the make of the television. Choose any well-known make that you like.
At the bottom of your advertisement, on the left-hand side of the page write in block capitals, 'CONTACT JOSEPHINE, that's J-O-S-E-P-H-I-N-E'.
After Josephine put a colon and then - in figures - two-six-two-double-three-oh-nine.

*(Wait thirty seconds and then read each instruction again **once** only.)*

PART THREE, PART THREE. *(Check that candidates have found PART 3.)*

A group of schoolchildren is coming to visit your town. You are waiting to hear some information about the group before they arrive. You will hear the information **once** only. Look at the form now. *(10 seconds)*

Ready? Now listen to the information and fill in the form.

Hope you're more or less ready for the schoolchildren who are coming to visit your school. There are sixteen pupils in the group. They all seem very pleasant. Their ages range from ten to fifteen - there's a pair of eleven-year old twins who you really can't tell apart and there are a couple of other pairs of brothers and sisters. There are ten girls and six boys. On the whole the boys are a bit older than the girls. They'll be arriving at the bus station on Monday the thirtieth of May at a quarter past ten. I'll come to the bus station to meet them too, if you like. They're going to be staying for four days and are really looking forward to their stay. Several of them have told me that they particularly want to visit the zoo, so do you think you'd be able to fit that into their programme somehow? They're travelling home by train. They're leaving early in the morning on Friday the third. Their train goes at half past five in the morning, I'm afraid. But if they didn't leave so early they wouldn't get home until long after midnight.
Ring me back if you need any more information at this stage.

(After reading the text wait 60 seconds.)

Stop writing, please.

You now have 2 hours 10 minutes to complete the rest of the paper.

Practice Test Three

PART ONE, PART ONE. *(Allow time to check that candidates have found PART 1.)*

In this first part you will hear ten sentences. Each sentence will be said **twice**. Choose the best reply for each one. Look at the example. *(15 seconds.)*

If you hear: 'What's the matter? You look very pale', the best answer is C. Put a circle round your answers.

Listen.

Number one, number one. *(5 seconds)*
Please leave your message after the tone.
Please leave your message after the tone. *(6 seconds)*

Number two, number two. *(5 seconds)*
Whereabouts in Britain does she live?
Whereabouts in Britain does she live? *(6 seconds)*

Number three, number three. *(5 seconds)*
Hello, how are things going?
Hello, how are things going? *(6 seconds)*

Number four, number four. *(5 seconds)*
I used to go to the cinema every Saturday.
I used to go to the cinema every Saturday. *(6 seconds)*

Number five, number five. *(5 seconds)*
How is your grandfather?
How is your grandfather? *(6 seconds)*

Number six, number six. *(5 seconds)*
What on earth did you do that for?
What on earth did you do that for? *(6 seconds)*

Number seven, number seven. *(5 seconds)*
How would you like your steak?
How would you like your steak? *(6 seconds)*

Number eight, number eight. *(5 seconds)*
Who does James live with?
Who does James live with? *(6 seconds)*

Number nine, number nine. *(5 seconds)*
I think I ought to be on my way.
I think I ought to be on my way. *(6 seconds)*

Number ten, number ten. *(5 seconds)*
I'm afraid I forgot to post your letter.
I'm afraid I forgot to post your letter. *(6 seconds)*

PART TWO, PART TWO. *(Allow time to check that candidates have found PART 2.)*

You are going to complete the map of Pitmanton by matching the various places of interest to their places on the map. Each number on the map represents one place of interest. Look at the map and the list of interesting places underneath. *(20 seconds)*

*(Read each instruction **twice** leaving ten seconds between instructions.)*

Ready? Now listen and complete the exercise. Write the numbers of the places of interest in the boxes beside the list of places. You will hear the instructions **twice**.

The smallest cafe in Britain is just in front of you as you come out of the railway station.
If you walk down Station Road and turn right and then go left, you will soon come to the Zoo on your left.
If you turn left at the end of Station Road and then take the second turning on your right you will find the Art Gallery at the end of that road on the right hand side.
Just opposite the Art Gallery is the Pitman Concert Hall.
The Theatre Royal is at the other end of town from the Art Gallery. It is right beside the river next to the Old Bridge.
The Victoria Theatre is in the town centre. It is on the north side of the Market Square.
On the west side of Market Square is the large Public Library.
The Archaeology Museum is next door to the Theatre Royal. It is a little further from the river than the theatre.

The Botanical Gardens are in the extreme south of the city.
The Local History Museum is not far from the Botanical Gardens. It is on Garden Road opposite the lake and just at the end of Station Road.

*(Give candidates thirty seconds and then read each instruction again **once** only.)*

PART THREE, PART THREE. *(Check that candidates have found PART 3.)*

You want to do a short English course in Britain. You would like to study for three weeks in August. You want to stay with an English family while you are doing the course. You are going to hear some information about three schools. Listen to the information and fill in the details asked for below. Then write down the name of the school which can give you the kind of course you want at the least expensive price. *(20 seconds)*

Ready? Now listen to the information and fill in the details. You will hear the information **once** only.

I've found out about three schools for you. They all seem quite good. First of all, there's the Queen's School of English. That does three- or four-week courses all through the year. From September to May the three-week courses cost five hundred pounds each. In the summer they're a hundred pounds more expensive, I'm afraid. Accommodation with an English family is extra, of course. It's eighty pounds a week. But they say that the Queen's School families are all friendly and treat their students like one of the family. Then there's the Princess School. It has lots of different courses. You pay a hundred and fifty pounds a week all through the year. Their family accommodation is a little bit cheaper too. It's only seventy-five pounds a week. There is just one problem with the Princess School. They don't have three-week courses in August, only four-week ones.
Finally I rang up the Duke School. It does have three-week courses in August. They cost five hundred and forty pounds. They can also arrange accommodation for students who want to live in families. Their family accommodation costs the same as that of the Princess School, seventy-five pounds a week. Oh no, sorry, it's an extra ten pounds a week in the summer.

Hope that's enough information to help you choose. Do ring me back if anything isn't clear.

(After reading the text wait 60 seconds.)

Stop writing, please.

You now have 2 hours 10 minutes to complete the rest of the paper.

Practice Test Four

PART ONE, PART ONE. *(Allow time to check that candidates have found PART 1.)*

In this first part you will hear ten sentences. Each sentence will be said **twice**. Choose the best reply for each one. Look at the example. *(15 seconds)*

If you hear: 'What's the matter? You look very pale', the best answer is C. Put a circle round your answers.

Listen.

Number one, number one. *(5 seconds)*
   What's the weather like there?
   What's the weather like there? *(6 seconds)*

Number two, number two. *(5 seconds)*
   What did you think of the film?
   What did you think of the film? *(6 seconds)*

Number three, number three. *(5 seconds)*
   May I use your phone?
   May I use your phone? *(6 seconds)*

Number four, number four. *(5 seconds)*
   I'm sorry I'm so late.
   I'm sorry I'm so late. *(6 seconds)*

Number five, number five. *(5 seconds)*
   Do you take sugar?
   Do you take sugar? *(6 seconds)*

Number six, number six. *(5 seconds)*
   How long does the flight take?
   How long does the flight take? *(6 seconds)*

Number seven, number seven. *(5 seconds)*
   I'm afraid she's out. Can I take a message?
   I'm afraid she's out. Can I take a message?
(6 seconds)

Number eight, number eight. *(5 seconds)*

Do you think it'd be a good idea to invite John too?
Do you think it'd be a good idea to invite John too?
(6 seconds)

Number nine, number nine. *(5 seconds)*

Could you tell me where the nearest phone box is, please?
Could you tell me where the nearest phone box is, please? *(6 seconds)*

Number ten, number ten. *(5 seconds)*

He may be some time. Do you want to wait?
He may be some time. Do you want to wait?
(6 seconds)

PART TWO, PART TWO. *(Allow time to check that candidates have found PART 2.)*

In your book you have a chart showing what is on at various cinemas and a list of the names of some films. Study the chart and the names of the films. *(30 seconds)*

*(Read each instruction **twice** leaving 10 seconds between the different instructions.)*

Ready? Now listen and complete the chart with the necessary information about cinemas, films, starting times and prices of tickets. You will hear each instruction **twice**.

The Odeon is showing *The Sound of Music*.
Casablanca starts at 7.30.
Shirley Valentine costs one pound more than *Casablanca*.
Rambo 6 is on at the ABC.
There is just one late showing. It is *Bride of Dracula* and it starts at midnight.
Before the *Bride of Dracula* at the same cinema you can see *ET*.
A ticket for the earlier show at the Regal costs three times as much as one for the children's cartoons.
The film at the Odeon Cinema begins fifteen minutes later than the one at the XYZ.
The children's cartoon films start at two forty-five.
A ticket for the ABC costs twice as much as one for the children's programme.

*(After reading wait for 30 seconds and then read the statements above again **once** only.)*

PART THREE, PART THREE. *(Allow time to check that candidates have found PART 3.)*

You are going to visit the old English city of York and a friend is recommending what you should see when you are there. You are interested only in history and you don't want to spend time shopping, sitting in cafes or walking in the countryside. Write down the places you should visit and make a note of any special things that you can see there. *(20 seconds)*

You will hear the information **once** only. Ready?

Yes, it's a great idea to visit York. There are masses of things you must try to do while you're there. First of all, of course, there's the Roman wall which still stands and goes round the old part of the city - you get some fantastic views of the town and it's particularly interesting to look at the ancient gates in the wall. There are other good walks in York itself especially along the banks of the river. There are some nice pubs and cafes beside the river and I'd certainly recommend stopping for refreshments as you walk.

There are some fantastic museums in York too. There's the Castle Museum, where you can see very lifelike reconstructions of old shops - you really get the feeling of having travelled back in time. Even better perhaps is the Viking Museum - that's spelt V-I-K-I-N-G - where you are shown what life was like in York a thousand or so years ago. Even the smells of those times have been re-created! Then there's a superb Transport Museum - there's a really interesting collection of old trains there.

York is also set in the middle of magnificent countryside. You can spend days walking in the hills not far from the city. So, don't forget your walking shoes. Oh, and I nearly forgot one of the best places of all - the old cathedral. The stained glass windows there are particularly famous and beautiful. Near the cathedral there are lots of interesting little shops - you should be able to buy some nice souvenirs there. I hope you have a marvellous trip. Don't forget to ring and tell me all about it when you get home.

(After reading the text wait 60 seconds.)

Stop writing, please.

You now have 2 hours 10 minutes to complete the rest of the paper.

Answers to Practice Tests

Practice Test One

Listening

Part 1

1	C		6	C
2	B		7	B
3	C		8	D
4	C		9	C
5	A		10	B

Part 2

The letters are illustrated in the following order. Top row from left to right: M,C,G,N. Middle row – X,A,T. Bottom row – H,U,S.

Part 3

Thursday July 6th, 1.35 p.m.; Vaakuna; train; 7th July, 1 p.m.; Friday July 14th; 4.10 p.m.; Tuesday July 18th; 2.45 p.m.; 071 683 5596; AGY 7203.

English Usage

1	was	6	like	11	possibly	16	in
2	died	7	whether	12	when	17	that
3	how	8	should	13	into	18	which
4	has	9	out	14	own	19	same
5	over	10	than	15	before	20	had

Reading One

1 C; 2 B; 3 A; 4 C; 5 C.

Reading Two

450, 150; 45, 15; 45, 30; 44, 22; 24, 24.

Reading Three

Society of Authors; The Old Man of Lochnagar; children's; A Vision of Britain; treatise against modern architecture; check contracts, cheap photocopying, financial help; 5,000; Winston Churchill, Douglas Hurd, Jeffrey Archer; Mark le Fanu; 1884.

Reading and Writing

There are many possible ways of answering this question. Here is one suggestion.

My suitcase was a large brown leather one with a red strap round it. The suitcase cost me £250 when I bought it. It was about two years old and I had only used it twice before. In it I had all my clothes for a fortnight in the USA. I had three pairs of jeans, two dresses, six or seven shirts, two jerseys and two skirts. I had a pair of boots and three pairs of shoes. I also, of course, had lots of underwear, socks and tights. There was my toilet bag and my hair dryer. It would cost me at least £800 to replace all these clothes. I had bought a lot of presents and souvenirs in the States and they were in the suitcase too. There were about six books about the USA, half a dozen cassettes, some American candy, three souvenir T-shirts and a bottle of Bourbon. The total value of all these presents and souvenirs must be about £200. I hope that this is all the information that you need but should be happy to provide more if required.

Writing

No model answers are given for this or for any other of the Writing questions in the Practice Tests. For an idea of the length and the complexity of the compositions expected of the best students at this level, see the model compositions provided at the end of the Intermediate Exam Help section.

Practice Test Two

Listening

Part 1

1	A	6	D
2	C	7	D
3	C	8	C
4	A	9	B
5	C	10	D

Part 2

* ONLY two years old.
* (Mitsubishi - or any other make of TV)
* <u>In good condition.</u>

TV FOR SALE
(Picture of TV)
Only £40!
CONTACT JOSEPHINE: 262 3309

Part 3

16; 10-15; 6; 10; Monday 30th May, 10.15; bus station; Friday 3rd June, 5.30 a.m.; railway station.

English Usage

1	used	6	still	11	like	16	possible
2	their	7	for	12	what	17	some
3	as	8	of	13	when	18	then
4	were	9	because	14	however	19	Although
5	them	10	from	15	in	20	next

Reading One

1 B; 2 D; 3 A; 4 B; 5 D.

Reading Two

The answers to be filled in from top to bottom are:
1822; became a reporter; 1834; 1836; 1836; *Oliver Twist* published; 1842; 1858; *A Tale of Two Cities* published; 1870.

Reading Three

1,6,10; 5,8; 2,7; 2,8; 3,4,5,9,11; 2,11; 2.

Reading and Writing

There are many possible ways of answering this question. Here is one suggestion.

I should like this money to go to help children because children are the future of the world. I would give it to a charity in my town which organises a nursery for children of single mothers. It allows the mothers to train for work so that they can provide a better life for their children. It gives the children a secure and friendly daytime atmosphere where they can learn lots of interesting new things and play with other children. I spent a week last summer helping in the nursery and was very impressed by the quality of loving care which the staff offer. The nursery exists thanks to donations from local people and it very much wants to be able to provide a better range of toys and learning opportunities for its children. £5000 would enable it to equip itself beyond its utmost dreams. Please let the money go to the Ragdoll Nursery. Its children would be so happy.

Writing

No model answers are given for this or for any other of the Writing questions in the Practice Tests. For an idea of the length and the complexity of the compositions expected of the best students at this level, see the model compositions provided at the end of the Intermediate Exam Help section.

Practice Test Three

Listening

Part 1

1	C	6	A
2	A	7	C
3	C	8	D
4	B	9	A
5	D	10	C

Part 2

10 - Victoria Theatre; 7 Theatre Royal; 4 Cafe; 1 Botanical Gardens; 8 Archaeology Museum; 2 Local History Museum; 6 Concert Hall; 9 Public Library; 3 Zoo; 5 Art Gallery.

Part 3

Queens – £600; £80 per week
Princess – £150 a week (no 3-week courses, only 4-week ones in August); £75.
Duke – £540; £85.
Duke.

English Usage

1	the	6	leaves	11	much	16	so
2	in	7	were	12	not	17	enough
3	numbers	8	much	13	themselves	18	same
4	how	9	of	14	trees	19	certain
5	They	10	However	15	each	20	may

Reading One

1 D; 2 A; 3 D; 4 C; 5 B.

Reading Two

Letters in order of frequency - e, t, a, o, i, n, s, r, h, l, d, c, u, m, f, p, g, w, y, b, v, k, x, j, q, z.

Reading Three

500,000; Testerton, 250,000; 700 miles, 700 miles; fishing, farming; bird-watching, botany, swimming, mountaineering; knitwear, tinned fish, Sogu (drink); Pitmanese; Binpall, 1,700 metres; Prison sentence for leaving litter, no development within 1 kilometre of water's edge, quota of 50 tourists per country per year.

Reading and Writing

There are many possible ways of answering this question. Here is one suggestion.

I think it would be best to come in September if you can as the weather is usually quite good then and also there are not too many tourists at that time. I would suggest that you start in Edinburgh and spend a day there exploring the old city. The next day you should drive through Stirling to the west coast. There are wonderful mountains and lakes there and you should have a wonderful time. If I were you I would spend a week based in a little place called Balmacara. There is a lovely hotel there and you can easily travel from there to lots of other interesting places if you want to do more touring. You must visit the island of Skye, for example, and, if you wanted, you could go to the far north of the country. It is very wild and beautiful there. In September there are lots of Highland Games in this area and you should be able to attend one of those. From Balmacara it is also easy to drive along Loch Ness – you might even see the Monster. You might also enjoy visiting a whisky distillery – but perhaps it would be better to go there by bus. Tours are organised from Fort William, which is not far from Balmacara. From Balmacara return south via Glasgow. Glasgow is a large industrial city but it also has some museums and art galleries which are well worth visiting. I'd spend a day there. I think that this should give you a great ten days holiday in Scotland and hope that it sounds all right to you.

Writing

No model answers are given for this or for any other of the Writing questions in the Practice Tests. For an idea of the length and the complexity of the compositions expected of the best students at this level, see the model compositions provided at the end of the Intermediate Exam Help section.

Listening

Part 1

1	C	6	B
2	B	7	A
3	A	8	B
4	D	9	C
5	C	10	D

Part 2

ABC – Rambo 6, £4; Odeon – Sound of Music, 8.15; Rex – 2.45; 7.30; XYZ – £5.50; Regal – ET, £6; Bride of Dracula.

Part 3

Roman wall – ancient gates (views); Castle Museum – old shops; Viking Museum – recreation of life 1,000 years ago (smells); Transport Museum – old trains; Cathedral – stained glass windows.

English Usage

1	also	6	by	11	better	16	So
2	are	7	much	12	Just	17	however
3	less	8	when	13	or	18	should
4	about	9	improvements	14	older	19	regularly
5	between	10	It	15	can	20	once

Reading One

1 B; 2 C; 3 B; 4 A; 5 C.

Reading Two

The points that need to be filled in on the pie-chart are underlined below:

32% - ladies' clothing; 29% - food; 20% – men's clothing; 1% – flowers; 1% – cosmetics; 6% – children's clothing; 5% – stationery; 4% – kitchen equipment; 3% – furnishing.

On the graph the figures should be as follows for each of the years indicated:

1981 $250,000; 1982 $275,000; 1983 $300,000; 1984 $360,000; 1985 $395,000; 1986 $450,000; 1987 $510,000; 1988 $561,000; 1989 $661,000; 1990 $750,000.

Reading Three

Answers from top to bottom are:

Japanese; small (fits into pocket or handbag); 320 grammes; 50 to 3,200; 1/60 to 1/500; Yes; grey; grey or red; every couple of years or about 400 flashes; £200.

Reading and Writing

There are many possible ways of answering this question. Here is one suggestion.

Dear Sirs,

I should very much like your computer to find me a penfriend. I should like to write to a girl of about my age – seventeen years old – from anywhere in the south of Europe: Greece, Italy or Spain, perhaps. I should like to write to someone who has similar interests to mine, if possible. I love sports, particularly water sports. I go swimming at least twice a week and have recently learnt to water-ski and to windsurf. I am not very good yet but I practise as often as possible. I am still at school and plan to go to university next year. I would like to study history. History is my favourite subject at school but I also like learning languages. I speak quite good French and a little Spanish. I live in a small town on the south coast of England with my parents and my twin sister. Apart from my sister, my best friend is my spaniel, Noddy.

    Yours faithfully,

    Sandra Smith

Writing

No model answers are given for this or for any other of the Writing questions in the Practice Tests. For an idea of the length and the complexity of the compositions expected of the best students at this level, see the model compositions provided at the end of the Intermediate Exam Help section.

Pitman ESOL Practice Tests – Higher Intermediate Level

Exam Help

Listening

p.8 ex. A

Answers

a Parents who think their little daughter is looking tired.
'Why don't you take her upstairs and read her a story.'

b Somebody who has just faced or is just facing some unpleasant experience.
'I didn't know it would be like this.'

c At a party; two people are talking about someone one of them does not know very well.
'He's a doctor, I think.'

d People indoors and one of them wants some fresh air.
'Shall I open the window?'

e Friends discussing other mutual friends.
'That's wonderful news.'

f People playing a game in which players take turns – monopoly, draughts or scrabble, for instance.
'Oh, have you been already?'

g Two people at home wondering if there's anything special on television that evening.
'There's a film I'd like to see on Channel 4 at 10 o'clock.'

h Someone checking a letter someone else has written or notes they have made in preparation for a speech.
'Why ever not?'

i Someone beginning to get angry about the thought that someone else might not be on time.
'I'm sure he won't.'

j A friend who has unexpectedly arrived in town and wants some accommodation.
'Yes, of course, if you don't mind a mattress on the floor?'

k Someone who thinks a friend is pulling their leg or teasing them.
'No, I'm absolutely serious.'

l Someone who wants permission to smoke.
'I'd rather you didn't.'

m Someone who has answered a business phone and tells you that the extension you want is engaged at the moment.
'No, I'll call back later.'

n Someone who thinks that someone else's behaviour is bad.
'Oh, I think she's been punished enough.'

o Someone who is really happy because their salary has just been increased.
'Congratulations. Let's go out and celebrate.'

p Someone who has seen or heard something that they find really unpleasant, even disgusting.
'Don't look at it then.'

p.9 ex. C

Answers

b exclamation mark; c comma; d full stop; e semi-colon; f colon; g inverted commas; h asterisk; i brackets; j hyphen; k apostrophe; l dash.

SUE is written in capital letters whereas Sue is written normally.

£25 is in figures whereas twenty-five pounds is written in full.

Friday is written in full whereas Fri. is an abbreviation or is abbreviated.

p.9 ex. D

Read the following instructions to the students. Read them at normal speaking speed and don't highlight anything to make it easier for the students.

a Write down just the names and ages of the children in the Jones family.
The Joneses have five kids. The oldest is Mark. He's 15 now, no he had a birthday last week, he must be 16 already. Next comes John. He's a couple of years younger, he'll be 14 in a couple of months' time. In the middle there's Anna, the only girl. She's just turned twelve. Richard and Jack are quite a bit younger. Richard's 6 and Jack's four years younger than he is.

Students should write Mark 16, John 13, Anna 12, Richard 6 and Jack 2.

b Write down the names of the hotels and their phone numbers.

I've found three hotels which I think might be good ones for you. You'll need to phone them, however, to find out if they've got rooms when you want them. The first is called the London and its phone number is 081 238 9946. The second one is The George and its number is 071 550 2368. The last one – and I think this one perhaps sounds the most promising – is the Central and its number is 071 729 0534.

Students should write London 081 238 9946, George 071 550 2368, Central 071 729 0534.

c Write notes of the three things you have to do.

Could you go into town and do a couple of jobs for me this afternoon. please. First could you buy me a copy of *Personal Computer* magazine. Make sure you get the July issue, I've already read the June one. Then, could you take these three films in to be developed. I'd like glossy prints and two sets of each, please, so I can send copies to grandma. Could you also take my black shoes to be repaired, please. It's just the heels which need doing and so you should be able to get them done while you wait.. Thanks a lot.

Students should write Buy July *Personal Computer*, Take films for developing (glossy prints, two sets), Repair black shoes (heels).

English Usage

p.10 Ten Weeks in a Life Raft
Answers

1	following	11	heat
2	ate	12	fresh, drinking
3	with	13	by
4	on	14	out
5	dorado	15	stove
6	which	16	piece
7	was	17	to
8	after	18	as
9	later	19	were
10	had	20	fit, unharmed

p.11 Japan
Answers

1	watch, see	11	cent
2	after, behind	12	crossing
3	off	13	even
4	there	14	at
5	of	15	least
6	to	16	away, off
7	about	17	does
8	fact	18	on, upon
9	densely	19	do
10	times	20	when, as

p.11 The Man in the Iron Mask
Answers

1	was	11	ending
2	only	12	most
3	wore	13	died
4	on	14	to
5	secret	15	to, for
6	to	16	Those
7	no	17	should
8	at, on	18	was
9	from	19	What
10	To	20	to

Reading One

pp.12-13 ex. A

Here you have the original words to fit the blanks and an explanation of why each of the options suggested cannot be correct.

1 The original words read 'how would he react'.
 a is wrong because it is not a question.
 b is wrong because there is no reference to a wife after the blank.
 c is wrong because it does not follow logically from the sentence before the blank.

2 The original words read 'the courier service, E-mail and faxes'.
 a is wrong because the whole text is about language rather than transport communications.
 b is wrong because postcards and greeting cards are older than the telephone and the telegram.
 c is wrong because the word 'these' in the next sentence will not then make sense.

3 The original words read 'And so are you'.
 a is wrong because 'jam' does not rhyme with 'blue'.
 b is wrong because it does not make much sense in the rhyme.
 c is wrong because the rhythm is wrong.

4 The original words read 'when you wish to sleep or to leave the compartment'.
 a is wrong because 'having a snooze' is too informal a style to fit the rest of the text.
 b is wrong because it would require a comma after 'doors'.
 c is wrong because there would have to be a comma both before and after this phrase.

Reading and Writing

p.14 ex. A

a The elements of the question which students should mark are: summer holiday, find a job, go away and have a good holiday, need a break, hard year at school, my parents want me to spend most of the summer studying, How can I persuade them that it's not really necessary to study this holiday?
 If students have marked other parts of the question, that does not really matter but all the above elements should be there.

b The elements of the question which students should mark are: young people today watch too much TV, hardly ever open a book, music they play is lacking in any lasting value, totally selfish and lacking in basic manners.

Writing

p.16 ex. C Two Model Compositions

There are, of course, many different ways of writing the compositions set. Here are a couple of suggestions. They are presented merely in order to give an idea of the length and complexity of writing which is expected of the best candidates at Pitman Higher Intermediate level.

Has your country been fortunate from a geographical point of view? Discuss the ways in which your country has been lucky or unlucky in terms of her climate, topography and natural resources.

My country is Britain and I think that, like most countries, she has in some ways been lucky and in some ways unlucky from a geographical point of view.

As far as climate is concerned, she has certainly been fortunate. Of course, people complain all the time about the weather in Britain but, geographically speaking, we are lucky in having a moderate climate. We do not have to cope with the extremes of climate which many places have. We have neither terribly cold winters nor desperately hot summers. We do not experience either really torrential rains or full-scale droughts. Our weather is mild and temperate; it may not be the best weather for lying on the beach but it is excellent for growing crops.

What about topography? We are lucky in that we have a rich variety of landscape within the boundaries of our small island. We are also fortunate to be an island. This has frequently stood us in good stead throughout our history. However, we could certainly do with more land. Much of the north of the country is inhospitable and is not suitable either as building land or for agriculture. The richer land of the south is already over-populated.

As far as natural resources go, we were extremely fortunate in the past to have plentiful supplies of iron ore and coal. This is what helped Britain to become the first industrial nation. However, we do not have such resources as gold or uranium which would nowadays be more valuable. There is some oil in the North Sea but not enough to provide us with real wealth.

All things considered, I would say that Britain has been geographically lucky. We may not have everything that we could wish for but we have been far more fortunate than many places.

What information and advice would you give to a friend who asks you what the Pitman Higher Intermediate exam is like and how he or she should prepare for it?

The Pitman Higher Intermediate exam is one of a series of five English exams set by the Pitman Examinations Institute. It is the second one from the top and so is quite difficult. It tests how well you can understand spoken English and how good you are at reading and writing English. You are allowed to use an English-English dictionary to help you if you wish.

The most difficult question, in my opinion, is the one called Listening Part Three. In this question you have to listen to something and make notes or do some other task based on what you hear. However, you hear the piece only once and so you really have to concentrate. Another quite tricky question is the English Usage one. Here you have to find which words fit twenty blanks in a text. I also find the Reading and Writing questions quite hard sometimes. In these questions you have to write something based on what you read – you might have to write an answer to a letter, for example. The difficult part here is remembering to include everything that the question asks you to do. You must read the question carefully and plan your answer before you start writing.

If you decide to take the exam, I would advise you to pay particular attention to those three types of question. Make sure that you do plenty of practice with such questions. It is also, of course, important to do some complete practice tests so that you know exactly what to expect in the examination. Last but not least, don't forget to read and to listen to as much English as you possibly can.

p.16 ex. D
The corrected sentences should read.
a Many people live in Tokyo and everybody is very polite.
b We have been living in this house for five years.
c If I had known, I would never have asked him to the party.
d There are many reasons for his strange behaviour.
e As soon as the bell goes, we shall all stop working.
f We first met when I was 18 years old.
g After making such an interesting journey, she'll now have to find a job.
h She got married to Dennis despite the fact that she didn't really love him / despite not really loving him.
i He has a lot of difficulty in understanding English grammar.
j They suggested we should visit / we visited them at the weekend.
k She did not know which of the bicycles he preferred.
l It was one of the best restaurants I have ever been to.
m There is a lot of interesting news today.
n The photo shows a beautiful young girl on the beach.
o It is very hard to get used to driving on the left in England.
p I hope you will all do well in your examination/I wish you all the best in your examination.

Listening Scripts

Practice Test One

PART ONE, PART ONE *(Allow time to check that candidates have found PART 1.)*

In this first part you will hear ten sentences. Each sentence will be said **twice.** Choose the best reply for each one. Look at the example. *(15 seconds)*

If you hear: 'What's the matter? You look very pale', the best answer is C. Put a circle round your answers.

Listen.

Number one, number one. *(5 seconds)*
How do you like your coffee?
How do you like your coffee?   *(10 seconds)*

Number two, number two. *(5 seconds)*
How's life?
How's life? *(10 seconds)*

Number three, number three. *(5 seconds)*
Cheer up. Things can't be that bad.
Cheer up. Things can't be that bad.   *(10 seconds)*

Number four, number four. *(5 seconds)*
Please keep this between ourselves.
Please keep this between ourselves. *(10 seconds)*

Number five, number five.   *(5 seconds)*
He should have known better.
He should have known better.   *(10 seconds)*

Number six, number six.   *(5 seconds)*
Have you got a light?
Have you got a light?   *(10 seconds)*

Number seven, number seven.   *(5 seconds)*
Did you invite him to the party?
Did you invite him to the party?   *(10 seconds)*

Number eight, number eight.   *(5 seconds)*
What's John doing this summer?
What's John doing this summer?   *(10 seconds)*

Number nine, number nine.   *(5 seconds)*
You must be joking.
You must be joking. *(10 seconds)*

Number ten, number ten.   *(5 seconds)*
Could you spare me a moment?
Could you spare me a moment?   *(10 seconds)*

PART TWO, PART TWO. *(Check that candidates have found PART 2.)*

In this part you are going to design an advertisement for a number of articles. Listen to the information and use what you hear to complete the advertisement. You may write notes as you listen. You will hear the information **twice.** *(10 seconds)*

Ready?

At the top of the box, in the middle, write – in capital letters – Articles for Sale.   *(6 seconds)*

Draw an asterisk at either end of what you have written. *(6 seconds)*

At the bottom of the page write – in ordinary handwriting – Contact Jane, colon, Telephone 230756. Abbreviate the word, telephone, giving it a capital letter, and put the telephone number in figures, of course. *(6 seconds)*

Down the left-hand side of the box write the numbers one to four. Space them evenly down the page. *(6 seconds)*

You are now going to write what is for sale beside each number. Remember to leave some space at the right-hand side of the page because you are going to write the prices of the articles there later.

Beside number one write – in capital letters – NEARLY NEW GOLD PEN.   *(6 seconds)*

At the bottom of the list write – in ordinary handwriting – English dictionary.   *(6 seconds)*

The article beside number three should also be written in capital letters. It should say 250-PIECE JIGSAW – that's J-I-G-S-A-W. Write the number in figures not words. *(6 seconds)*

In the remaining slot on the list write – but not in capitals – black leather briefcase. *(6 seconds)*

63

All you have to do now is write the prices after each article. Write these in figures. After the first item on the list put ten pounds. *(6 seconds)*

The next item on the list costs half as much as the first one. *(6 seconds)*

The second last item on the list costs only fifty p. and the remaining item is just twice that amount. *(6 seconds)*

Put an exclamation mark after each price and your advertisement is now complete.

(Allow 15 seconds before reading the instructions for a second time.)

Now I'll read the instructions again. *(Read the instructions again.)*

(Allow a further 30 seconds before going on to PART 3.)

PART THREE, PART THREE. *(Check that candidates have found PART 3.)*

You and a friend are interested in going to the cinema this evening. You will not be free until six o'clock and so you cannot go to anything in the afternoon. You have to get up early in the morning and so you don't want to go to a late-night performance either. Listen to the recorded cinema information and complete the table with information about the evening films only – not the afternoon ones and not the late-night ones. Look at the form now. *(15 seconds)* Now listen and complete the form. You will hear the information **once** only.

Ready?

This is a recorded announcement about the films showing in Higherton at the moment. There are a lot of good films on in Higherton this week. First of all for children at two o'clock at the ABC cinema there's a showing of the Walt Disney classic cartoon, *Snow White and the Seven Dwarfs*. Also at the ABC but in the evening at seven thirty there's a film for adults. It's the film version of the romantic musical, *True Love*. So that's *True Love* starting promptly at seven thirty. In sharp contrast to *True Love*, the late-night showing at the ABC is a thriller, *Vampires*. That starts appropriately enough at midnight. The Rex Cinema has no matinee this week but at eight o'clock you can see one of the most popular Westerns ever made, *High Noon*. If you haven't seen it before you mustn't miss *High Noon*, showing at eight at the Rex all this week. Finally we come to the Queen's Cinema. The Queen's has no matinee either this week but at eight fifteen you can see the new film, *Murder on Fifth Avenue*. As its name suggests, *Murder on Fifth Avenue* is a detective story. It'll have you sitting on the edge of your seats as will the late-night screening of *Dracula and Frankenstein*. This is also on at the Queen's at half past eleven. If you would like further information about any of these films, call 253461, that's 253461. Thank you for calling.

You now have three minutes to complete your answer.

You now have 2 hours 10 minutes to complete the rest of the paper.

Practice Test Two

PART ONE, PART ONE. *(Allow time to check that candidates have found PART 1.)*

In this first part you will hear ten sentences. Each sentence will be said twice. Choose the best reply for each one. Look at the example. *(15 seconds)*

If you hear: 'What's the matter? You look very pale', the best answer is C. Put a circle round your answers.

Listen.

Number one, number one. *(5 seconds)*
How long have you been here?
How long have you been here? *(10 seconds)*

Number two, number two. *(5 seconds)*
My feet are killing me.
My feet are killing me. *(10 seconds)*

Number three, number three. *(5 seconds)*
He'd better not be late.
He'd better not be late. *(10 seconds)*

Number four, number four.   *(5 seconds)*
Did Mary marry <u>James</u>?
Did Mary marry <u>James</u>?   *(10 seconds)*

Number five, number five.   *(5 seconds)*
Let's try and put them off.
Let's try and put them off.   *(10 seconds)*

Number six, number six.   *(5 seconds)*
Have you got any spare 10p.s?
Have you got any spare 10p.s?   *(10 seconds)*

Number seven, number seven.   *(5 seconds)*
Could I leave her a message please?
Could I leave her a message please?   *(10 seconds)*

Number eight, number eight.   *(5 seconds)*
What did you do that for?
What did you do that for?   *(10 seconds)*

Number nine, number nine.   *(5 seconds)*
Have you got used to him yet?
Have you got used to him yet?   *(10 seconds)*

Number ten, number ten.   *(5 seconds)*
I'm dying for a cup of tea.
I'm dying for a cup of tea.   *(10 seconds)*

PART TWO, PART TWO. *(Check that the candidates
have found PART 2.)*

Look at your book. You are going to draw a table,
giving some amusing or interesting information about
the British and their beliefs and habits. You will hear
some instructions to help you complete the table. You
may take notes as you listen. Write the percentages in
figures and the facts in note form.   *(10 seconds)*

Ready? You will hear the instructions **twice.**

95% of Britons say they like winter.   *(6 seconds)*
87% of British high earners are men.   *(6 seconds)*
82% of the British population said they had read a book
in 1987. *(6 seconds)*
66.3% of Britons agree that their family is more
important to them than their career. *(6 seconds)*
63% of British housewives claim that their husbands
help with the washing-up most days, whereas 73% of
British husbands claim that they do so. *(6 seconds)*
32% of British teachers say that they have been

physically attacked by a pupil. *(6 seconds)*
30% of British adult females have no natural teeth. *(6
seconds)*
13% of British adults think they know the name of their
Euro-MP – but 5% of those got it wrong. *(6 seconds)*
1.1% of the British working population is in the Armed
Forces.

*(Allow fifteen seconds before reading the instructions
for a second time.)*

Now I'll read the instructions again. *(Read the
instructions again.)*

*(Allow a further thirty seconds before going on to PART
3.)*

PART THREE, PART THREE. *(Check that the
candidates have found PART 3.)*

Look at the map. You are going to visit a friend.
Listen to the instructions. Draw the route on the
map. Also mark your friend's house with a cross.
Roads in Britain usually have an A or B number,
for example, the A4 or the B22. Write the
numbers of any roads that the speaker mentions
beside the appropriate road on the map. Look at
the map now. *(15 seconds)* You will hear the
information **once** only.

Ready?

Leave Pitmanbridge by the A3 going north. You
cross a railway bridge and then take the second
turning on the left. It's the B45, I think. Go
along the B45 for about a mile or so. You'll pass
two turnings on your left and then take the next
road that you come to on your right. It's the B607.
You cross the river fairly soon after you turn into
the B607. Go along the B607 for about three
miles. You come to a little village with a pretty
church and three pubs. The A62 goes through this
village crossing the B607. You go straight across
the A62 but you take the next turning on your
right. That'll be the B669. Our house is about
two miles along the road. It's on the left-hand side
of the road fairly soon after you cross the railway.
If you come to a cross-roads you've gone too far.

Our house is about halfway between the railway bridge and the cross-roads, in fact. Hope all this is clear. Give us a ring if you get lost.

You now have three minutes to complete your answer.

You now have 2 hours 10 minutes to complete the rest of the paper.

Practice Test Three

PART ONE, PART ONE. *(Allow time to check that candidates have found PART 1.)*

In this first part you will hear ten sentences. Each sentence will be said twice. Choose the best reply for each one. Look at the example. *(15 seconds)*

If you hear: 'What's the matter? You look very pale', the best answer is C. Put a circle round your answers.

Listen.

Number one, number one. *(5 seconds)*
Whereabouts do you live?
Whereabouts do you live? *(10 seconds)*

Number two, number two. *(5 seconds)*
I'll pick you up at seven.
I'll pick you up at seven. *(10 seconds)*

Number three, number three. *(5 seconds)*
Did Jill speak to Ben <u>yesterday</u>?
Did Jill speak to Ben <u>yesterday</u>? *(10 seconds)*

Number four, number four. *(5 seconds)*
You could have rung.
You could have rung. *(10 seconds)*

Number five, number five. *(5 seconds)*
Would you like a second helping?
Would you like a second helping? *(10 seconds)*

Number six, number six. *(5 seconds)*
Is this seat taken?
Is this seat taken? *(10 seconds)*

Number seven, number seven. *(5 seconds)*
Can I borrow your newspaper?
Can I borrow your newspaper? *(10 seconds)*

Number eight, number eight. *(5 seconds)*
I'd rather we didn't stay here much longer.
I'd rather we didn't stay here much longer. *(10 seconds)*

Number nine, number nine. *(5 seconds)*
She will keep asking such silly questions.
She will keep asking such silly questions. *(10 seconds)*

Number ten, number ten. *(5 seconds)*
Where on earth did you get those boots?
Where on earth did you get those boots? *(10 seconds)*

PART TWO, PART TWO. *(Allow time to check the candidates have found PART 2.)*

You will hear some instructions which you must follow in order to complete the diagrams. You may write notes as you listen. The diagrams tell you about the senior staff of a Sports Hall. You will hear the instructions **twice.**

Ready?

Write Senior staff in block capitals above diagram A. *(6 seconds)*

Write the name, Jocelyn Wilcox, in the top box. That's J-O-C-E-L-Y-N W-I-L-C-O-X. *(6 seconds)*
Miss Wilcox's deputy is Robert Johnstone, that's Johnstone with a T and an E. Write his name and his title, that's Deputy Director, in the appropriate box. *(6 seconds)*
Bill Craig is Health and Safety Officer. Add his title to the box where you see his name. *(6 seconds)*
Jack Brown has special responsibility for the swimming pool. Write his name, Jack Brown without an E, in the appropriate box. *(6 seconds)*
The final member of the senior team is known as the Children's Officer. Her name is Rosemary Hill. Write her name and title in the bottom right-hand box. *(6 seconds)*

Now write the initials, the initials only, of the senior staff in their offices. *(6 seconds)*
The Director's Office is the large office immediately to your right as you enter the sports hall. *(6 seconds)*
The Swimming Pool Director has his office next to the pool. *(6 seconds)*

The Deputy Director's office is between the Swimming Pool Director's office and the Health and Safety Officer's office. *(6 seconds)*

The Children's Officer is based in the office opposite Jocelyn Wilcox's office.

(Allow fifteen seconds before reading the instructions for a second time.)

Now I'll read the instructions again. *(Read the instructions again.)*

(Allow a further thirty seconds before going on to PART 3.)

PART THREE, PART THREE. *(Allow time to check that the candidates have found PART 3.)*

You are staying in a friend's house while he is on holiday. He is going to phone you soon to find out if there are any messages on his answer phone. Listen to the messages on his answer phone for him and make notes about the different calls. *(15 seconds)* You will hear the information **once** only.

Ready?

Hi, it's John here, John Brown. I hate talking to these machines but this is quite important. Could you please call me back as soon as possible. I've got some information about a motorbike that I think you might be interested in buying. In case you've lost my number it's Oxford, that's 0865, 33487, that's 0865 33487.

Hello, this is Mary, Mary Grimshaw, that's G-R-I-M-S-H-A-W. I'm ringing from the City Council Offices with some news about your application for a summer job here. We can in fact probably offer you a selection of jobs but we need to discuss a few things fairly urgently. Could you please call me back any morning before one o'clock. The Council number is 263986 and I'm on extension 332.

Good morning, I believe you called my office last week but I was on holiday. I'm James Clarke, that's Clarke with an E at the end, from the Electricity Board. If you still need to get in touch then I'll give you a different number to use this month. It's 674522. In four weeks'

time it'll be better to use the number you used last week – in other words 445522 – again. Hope that's clear. Goodbye.

Practice Test Four

PART ONE, PART ONE. *(Allow time to check that candidates have found PART 1.)*

In this first part you will hear ten sentences. Each sentence will be said twice. Choose the best reply for each one. Look at the example. *(15 seconds)*

If you hear: 'What's the matter? You look very pale', the best answer is C. Put a circle round your answers.

Listen.

Number one, number one. *(5 seconds)*
It's time he had his hair cut.
It's time he had his hair cut. *(10 seconds)*

Number two, number two. *(5 seconds)*
What did you make of him?
What did you make of him? *(10 seconds)*

Number three, number three. *(5 seconds)*
They've called off their wedding.
They've called off their wedding. *(10 seconds)*

Number four, number four. *5 seconds)*
Let's get a take-away tonight.
Let's get a take-away tonight. *(10 seconds)*

Number five, number five. *(5 seconds)*
Did <u>you</u> and Bob go to the theatre together last weekend?
Did <u>you</u> and Bob go to the theatre together last weekend? *(10 seconds)*

Number six, number six. *(5 seconds)*
He hasn't been feeling himself recently.
He hasn't been feeling himself recently. *(10 seconds)*

Number seven, number seven. *(5 seconds)*
Have you got any spare time this week?
Have you got any spare time this week? *(10 seconds)*

Number eight, number eight. *(5 seconds)*
When are you seeing the director?
When are you seeing the director? *(10 seconds)*

Number nine, number nine. *(5 seconds)*
He must have known she'd be furious.
He must have known she'd be furious. *(10 seconds)*

Number ten, number ten. *(5 seconds)*
It's rather chilly in here.
It's rather chilly in here. *(10 seconds)*

PART TWO, PART TWO. *(Allow time to check that the candidates have found PART 2.)*

You are going to design a poster for an event which a local English Club is organising. You are going to hear some information to help you design the poster. Listen to the information and complete the poster. You may take notes as you listen. You will hear the instructions **twice**. *(10 seconds)*

Ready?

In the middle of the box write Concert in large capital letters. *(6 seconds)*
Underneath Concert write the date of a week from today including both the day and the date. Do not abbreviate the name of the day. *(6 seconds)*
Underneath the date write Starts at seven thirty. Put the time in figures. *(6 seconds)*
Across the top of the box write – in ordinary handwriting – English dash American dash traditional dash pop. *(6 seconds)*
Below the first A in American draw three asterisks one below the other. *(6 seconds)*
Beside the first asterisk write Listen with an exclamation mark. *(6 seconds)*
Beside the second asterisk write Join in also with an exclamation mark. *(6 seconds)*
Beside the third asterisk write Enjoy traditional English refreshments in the interval. *(6 seconds)*
Draw a little picture of a cup of tea – with a saucer – underneath the note about refreshments. *(6 seconds)*
At the bottom of the notice write At colon and then The City Hall.

(Allow fifteen seconds before reading the instructions for a second time.)

Now I'll read the instructions again. *(Read the instructions again.)*

(Allow a further thirty seconds before going on to PART 3.)

PART THREE, PART THREE. *(Allow time to check that the candidates have found PART 3.)*

Study the notices that appeared in the Goods for Sale column of a local newspaper. You will hear a description of an item that is for sale. Listen to the description and then write a similar advertisement. You will hear the description **once** only. *(20 seconds)*

Ready?

Do you think you could possibly put an advert in the paper for me. I want to sell my camera. I don't need it now because my brother's given me a new one which is a bit more sophisticated. Still I can honestly say that it's in very good condition. It's only two years old, after all, and I've certainly had no problems with it. It's a Pentax, that's spelt P-E-N-T-A-X, and I suppose you'd better mention that it's an SLR. That stands for single lens reflex, of course, but the abbreviation should be fine in the ad. I find it's a very convenient camera because it's got a built-in flash though I dare say professionals prefer something separate. It's also got a telephoto lens which I've found enormously useful. I think it's worth a good sixty pounds. Put sixty pounds in the ad, anyhow, and we'll see what happens. Perhaps it'd be best if you give my mother's phone number as she's at home most of the time. That's 453980, 453980. OK? Thanks a lot for arranging this for me.

You now have five minutes to complete your advertisement.

You now have 2 hours 10 minutes to complete the rest of the paper.

Answers to Practice Tests

Practice Test One

Listening

Part 1

1	B	6	A
2	A	7	C
3	D	8	C
4	C	9	C
5	B	10	D

Part 2

```
                    * ARTICLES FOR SALE *


   1    NEARLY NEW GOLD PEN          £10!


   2    Black leather briefcase      £5!


   3    250-PIECE JIGSAW             50p!


   4    English dictionary           £1!


        Contact Jane: Tel.230756
```

Part 3

Name of film	Cinema	Performance starts at	Type of film
True Love	ABC	7.30	Romantic musical
High Noon	Rex	8.00	Western
Murder on Fifth Avenue	Queen's	8.15	Detective

English Usage

1	with	11	so, thus
2	to	12	the
3	down	13	the
4	have	14	At
5	is	15	is
6	Another	16	other
7	to	17	it
8	to	18	reaches
9	and, with	19	temperature
10	been	20	as

Reading One

1 C; 2 B; 3 A; 4 B; 5 C.

Reading Two

2 Rossetti Block
3 Palmer Block
4 Millais Block
5 Croquet Lawn
6 Perfumed Garden
7 Reynolds Block
8 Whistler Block
9 Rock Garden
10 TV Lounge
11 Tea Room
12 Function Hall
13 Library
14 Writing Room
15 Music Room
16 Turner Conference Room
17 Constable Conference Room
18 Hogarth Conference Room
19 Gainsborough Conference Room
20 Bar
21 Coffee lounge
22 Open air swimming pool
23 Tennis court
24 Car park
25 Main entrance, Reception

Reading Three

Age	Gross Motor	Manipulation	Understanding	Speech
28 weeks	1 Sits using hands for support. 2 Rolls from back to front.	1 Puts everything in mouth. 2 Bangs objects on table.	1 Responds to name. 2 May copy movements e.g. tongue protrusion.	Says 'Da', 'Ba', 'Ka'.
1 year	Walks with one hand held.	1 Rolls ball. 2 Gives and takes toy in play.	1 Interested in pictures in book. 2 Responds to 'Where is your shoe?'	Says two or three words with meaning.
21 months	1 Walks upstairs using two feet per step. 2 Picks up object from floor without falling.	1 Builds tower of five or six cubes. 2 Turns pages of books.	1 Pulls people to attract attention. 2 Points to parts of body on request.	1 Joins two words together. 2 Repeats things said.

Reading and Writing

The following points are those which must be included or taken account of in a successful candidate's answer:
> a suggestion for a middle-aged lady's tour of the candidate's country remembering that –
> tour to start at airport
> travelling by car
> only for ten days
> interest in history
> enjoyment of walking in countryside – lady wants to spend a couple of days doing this
> no interest in beaches or nightlife
> general advice for middle-aged lady travelling alone in candidate's country.

Writing

No model answer is provided for any of these compositions. If you wish to gain an impression of the length and degree of complexity expected of the best candidates at this level, look at the two model compositions provided at the end of the Higher Intermediate Exam Help section.

Practice Test Two

Listening

Part 1

1	C	6	C
2	B	7	D
3	C	8	C
4	D	9	D
5	A	10	C

Part 2

Percentage	Fact
95%	Britons say they like winter
87%	British high-earners are men
82%	Britons said they'd read a book in 1987
66.3%	Britons say family more important than career
63%	British women say husbands help with washing-up most days
73%	British husbands say they help with washing-up most days
32%	British teachers say they have been physically attacked by a pupil
30%	British adult females have no natural teeth
13%	British adults claim to know the name of their Euro-MP but 5% of those got it wrong.
1.1%	British working population is in Armed Forces

No marks are deducted for incorrect spelling or grammar here if the meaning of the fact is clear and correct.

Part 3

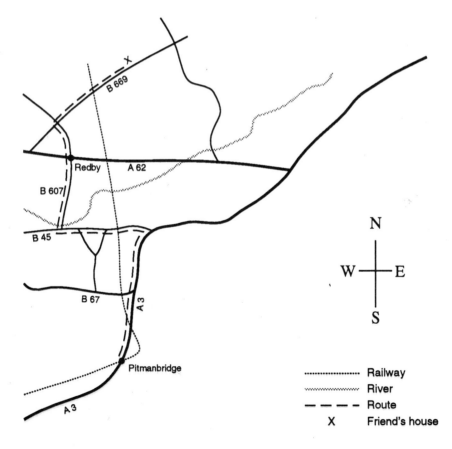

English Usage

1	all	11	himself
2	was	12	begun / started
3	much	13	take / make
4	way, manner	14	went
5	son	15	hard / difficult
6	had	16	good
7	to	17	consequently
8	given	18	when
9	to	19	built
10	death	20	be

Reading One

1 A; 2 B; 3 D; 4 A; 5 B.

Reading Two

North America
        Transport
        Physical Geography
        Industry and Agriculture
Asia
        Physical Geography
        Transport
        Industry and Agriculture
Europe
        Physical Geography
        Transport
        Twentieth Century Developments
South America
        Transport
        Physical Geography
        Industry and Agriculture
Africa
        Physical Geography
        Transport
        Twentieth Century Developments
Australia
        Physical Geography
        Transport
        Twentieth Century Developments
Antarctica
        Physical Geography
        Explorations
Appendix – Climatic Information
Appendix – Cities and Populations
Bibliography
Index

Reading Three

a) Computers can do many difficult things e.g.
1 play chess
2 produce new proofs in maths
3 read and translate a language

b) It can't do other things which people find easy e.g.
1 learn to speak a language
2 recognise simple items

c) Differences between the organisation of the human brain and computers:
   Human Brain
1 network of cells or neurons
2 each neuron connected to about 10,000 others
3 all neurons function at same time

   Computers
1 individual logic circuits
2 each circuit only linked to one other
3 each circuit works one after the other

d) Computers are better than brains at some things e.g
1 complex maths calculations

e) Neural networks differ from ordinary computers in that:
1 circuits wired up differently with lots of connections between them
2 they are programmed differently

f) Examples of neural networks:
        Where it is
1 Imperial College London
2 John Hopkins University Baltimore
3 Japan

        What it can do
1 can recognise a human smile
2 can pronounce words typed on a keyboard
3 can recognise Japanese characters

Reading and Writing

The following points are those which must be included in a successful candidate's answer:

opposition to the idea of life being peaceful without the telephone

objection to the thought that life would be better without the TV

objection to the suggestion that young people do not know how to talk properly

some appreciation of the variety in a supermarket

some suggestions as to how travel has improved

Writing

No model answer is provided for any of these compositions. If you wish to gain an impression of the length and degree of complexity expected of the best candidates at this level, look at the two model compositions provided at the end of the Higher Intermediate Exam Help section.

| Practice Test Three |

Listening

Part 1

1	A	6	A
2	B	7	B
3	A	8	C
4	C	9	D
5	C	10	B

Part 2

Diagram A
SENIOR STAFF

Jocelyn Wilcox
Director

Robert Johnstone
Deputy Director

Bill Craig
Health and Safety Officer

Jack Brown
Swimming Pool Director

Rosemary Hill
Children's Officer

Diagram B
The offices on the left-hand side from top to bottom should be labelled JB, RJ, BC and RH. The office on the right-hand side should be labelled JW.

Part 3

Call John Brown asap about a motorbike to buy. 0865 33487

Mary Grimshaw, City Council. Re application for summer job. Several possibilities. Call back asap (morning before 1 p.m.) 263986 ext. 332

James Clarke, Electricity Board. You rang last week – he was on holiday. If need him this month ring 674522 (new number). After four weeks he'll be back at old number (445522)

English Usage

1	US	11	arrive
2	to	12	if
3	either	13	thing
4	for	14	worse
5	crossing / flying	15	fact
6	be	16	but
7	be	17	might / would
8	not	18	To
9	on	19	before / until
10	for	20	nowhere

Reading One

1 C; 2 B; 3 C; 4 C; 5 D.

Reading Two

Position on list	Airport	Country / State	Number of passengers per year
1	Chicago O'Hare	Illinois	54,300,000
2	Atlanta	Georgia	45,000,000
3	Los Angeles	California	41,500,000
4	Dallas, Fort Worth	Texas	40,000,000
5	Heathrow, London	UK	34,700,000
6	Denver	Colorado	34,695,000
7	Newark	New Jersey	29,720,000
8	San Francisco	California	28,720,000
9	New York, JFK	New York	27,220,000
10	Tokyo	Japan	27,200,000

Reading Three

p.58
top left – c
top right – n
middle left – d
middle in the centre – a
middle right – j
bottom left – i
bottom centre – e
bottom right – extra picture (bagpipes)

p.59
top – g
second from the top – h
middle left – k
middle in the centre - f
middle right – l
bottom left – b
bottom centre – m
bottom right – o

Basic group of instruments	Two examples of that group
Woodwind	Any two of the following – saxophone, clarinet, flute, recorder, oboe, cor anglais, bassoon
Brass	trumpet, trombone
String	Any two of the following – violin, guitar, harp, zither, piano
Percussion	Any two of the following – castanets, cymbals, drum, xylophone

Reading and Writing

The following points are those which must be included in a successful candidate's answer:

four paragraphs, one about each of the people or pairs of people

each paragraph should suggest an appropriate film for that person or couple

it should also explain why that suggestion is felt to be appropriate

There are no right answers here but the following films might well be felt to be appropriate for the people concerned:

Love and Louisa for the Aitkens, a romantic and happy film for their wedding anniversary.

Brazil by Bike for Jane and Tom. Jane should find it appropriately educational and Tom might enjoy the bike bits.

Crime and Punishment for Susie and Ronnie because of their interest in history and their enjoyment of detective stories.

Splashdance for Ron, something light and amusing to cheer him up when he is feeling lonely.

Writing

No model answer is provided for any of these compositions. If you wish to gain an impression of the length and degree of complexity expected of the best candidates at this level, look at the two model compositions provided at the end of the Higher Intermediate Exam Help section.

Practice Test Four

Listening

Part 1

1	D	6	C
2	B	7	B
3	A	8	A
4	D	9	D
5	B	10	A

Part 2

English – American – traditional – pop
* Listen!
* Join in!
* Enjoy traditional English refreshments in the interval.

CONCERT
(date a week later than current date)
Starts at 7.30

At: The City Hall

Part 3

CAMERA   Pentax SLR. Built-in flash. Telephoto lens. Good condition. Only 2 years old. £60. Ring 453980.

English Usage

1	with	11	to
2	but	12	to
3	made / built	13	after
4	is	14	it
5	of	15	like
6	was	16	If
7	which	17	now
8	about	18	into
9	high	19	being
10	some / most / all	20	to

Reading One

1 B; 2 A; 3 C; 4 A; 5 D.

Reading Two

Under the table 3 = education; 5 = science.

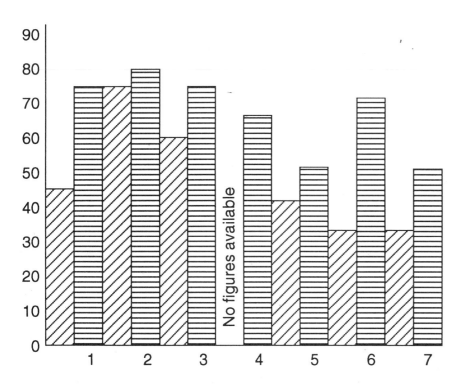

Reading Three

	Product	Ave. consumption
1	milk and cream	135
2	potatoes	112
3	beer	108
4	fruit	91
5	vegetables	85
6	grain products	70
7	meat	56
8	sugar, glucose and honey	44
9	oils and fats	22
10	eggs	13

Reading and Writing

The following points are those which must be included in a successful candidate's answer:

a more optimistic view of life in the future

some positive aspects of technology, perhaps

a defence of human nature

opposition to the idea that people will not get as much pleasure from life as now

Writing

No model answer is provided for any of these compositions. If you wish to gain an impression of the length and degree of complexity expected of the best candidates at this level, look at the two model compositions provided at the end of the Higher Intermediate Exam Help section.

Pitman ESOL Practice Tests – Advanced Level

Exam Help

Listening

p.7 ex. 1

Sentences to read to the students. The letter of the appropriate response is given in brackets after each sentence.)

1. I feel absolutely shattered.   (c)
2. She'd better get here on time.   (f)
3. Why don't we take a break now?   (a)
4. I wish they'd get on with it, don't you?   (g)
5. She isn't really cut out to be an athlete.   (e)
6. It's a bit stuffy in here, isn't it?   (b)
7. What a glorious view.   (h)
8. You're pulling my leg.   (d)
9. Do you fancy a night out?   (i)

English Usage

p. 9

Answers

1	not / never	11	for
2	when	12	as
3	that	13	do / can
4	what	14	of
5	by	15	beat
6	own	16	who
7	of	17	made
8	was	18	youngest
9	was	19	was, became
10	with	20	at, when

p.10 ex. 1

The correct answers to fit the blanks are given below but students may suggest possibilities that are just as valid.

a   The boy looks like a typical fifteen-year -old
b   cooking, waiting at table and serving drinks
c   Monkeys   57
d   it is a long journey from the nearest airport
e   Take all the appropriate equipment with you.

Model Compositions

A model answer is given for the Reading and Writing question and for one of the compositions in Practice Test One. This is to show the length and the kind of writing expected of the best candidates at this level.

Listening Scripts

Practice Test One

PART ONE, PART ONE. *(Allow time to check that candidates have found PART 1.)*

In this first part you will hear ten sentences. Each sentence will be said **twice.** Choose the best reply for each one. Look at the example. *(15 seconds)*

If you hear: 'What's the matter? You look very pale', the best answer is C. Put a circle round your answers.

Listen.

Number one, number one. *(5 seconds)*
I'm starving.
I'm starving. *(10 seconds)*

Number two, number two. *(5 seconds)*
You might have asked me first.
You might have asked me first. *(10 seconds)*

Number three, number three. *(5 seconds)*
Three cheers for Maria.
Three cheers for Maria. *(10 seconds)*

Number four, number four. *(5 seconds)*
However did you manage that?
However did you manage that? *(10 seconds)*

Number five, number five. *(5 seconds)*
Let's try and sort things out once and for all.
Let's try and sort things out once and for all. *(10 seconds)*

Number six, number six. *(5 seconds)*
Would you like to wash your hands?
Would you like to wash your hands? *(10 seconds)*

Number seven, number seven . *(5 seconds)*
It's a bit muggy today, isn't it.
It's a bit muggy today, isn't it. *(10 seconds)*

Number eight, number eight. *(5 seconds)*
I think we should get rid of these books now.
I think we should get rid of these books now. *(10 seconds)*

Number nine, number nine. *(5 seconds)*
Fancy meeting you here.
Fancy meeting you here. *(10 seconds)*

Number ten, number ten. *(5 seconds)*
It's up to you now.
It's up to you now. *(10 seconds)*

PART TWO, PART TWO. *(Check that candidates have found PART 2.)*

You are going to hear some information about four seaside cottages which are to rent. This information wil enable you to complete the chart below. You will hear the information **twice.** First study the chart.

(Allow 15 seconds for the students to look at the chart.)

I'm now going to read out the instructions which you must follow in order to complete the chart correctly. You will hear the instructions **twice.**

(Read the instructions at normal reading speed allowing 10 seconds between each instruction.)

1 Seaview is situated in a village called Flixton. That's F-L-I-X-T-O-N.
2 Ivy Retreat is in Aldeburgh, that's A-L-D-E-B-U-R-G-H.
3 Seaview can sleep six people, that's twice as many as Rose Cottage can cope with.
4 Rose Cottage is in the same village as Seaview whereas Journey's End is in the same village as Ivy Retreat.
5 Ivy Retreat can sleep four adults plus a baby because a cot is available there.
6 Journey's End is the largest cottage. It can manage eight people. No baby's cot is provided there, however.
7 Journey's End is also the most expensive at £250 per week in summer but it has some pretty special features: antique furniture, a dishwasher and so on.
8 Seaview is much cheaper at only half the cost of Journey's End but it also has some quite good features. The cottage is 300 years old and it's only 400 metres from the beach.
9 Rose Cottage is the only cottage with a telephone. The number of the cottage is 0231 956.

10 Ivy Retreat costs the same as Seaview. It's not so
close to the sea but it has a small swimming pool
and a tennis court in its garden.
11 Rose Cottage is the cheapest accommodation at
£115 per week.

*(Allow candidates 15 seconds and then repeat the
instructions.)*

PART THREE, PART THREE. *(Check that candidates
have found PART 3.)*

Look at the information sheet about a conference on
The English Language Today. You are going to listen
to part of Dr Johnson's welcome talk and will have to
make some changes to the programme in accordance
with the instructions you will hear. Make all the
necessary changes on the information sheet below.

(1 minute)

Ready? You will hear the instructions **once** only.

Welcome, ladies and gentlemen. It is very encouraging
to see so many of you here today. I hope that you will
all enjoy the conference and find it useful and
stimulating. First of all, I need to tell you about some
changes to the programme and I think it would be a
good idea if you marked those changes on the
programme which we sent you in advance. That should
avoid confusion later on.

First of all, tonight's keynote speech by Professor
Hammer will begin at eight rather than seven thirty.
That should allow us all more time to chat over dinner.

There is a third alternative on offer now as a
workshop tomorrow morning. Let's call that
group C. This workshop is to be called It's not
what you say, it's the way that you say it. Let me
repeat It's not what you say, it's the way that you
say it.

As you might expect from the title, Workshop C
will be dealing with pronunciation. It's going to
be in Seminar Room 35 and will be led by Anne
Cox, that's Anne with an E, C-O-X.

To allow you to sleep on the important decision of
which workshop to opt for, we've extended the

deadline for informing the Main Desk about your
choice. But we would ask you to choose and let
the Desk know about your decision before
breakfast tomorrow morning, that is before 8 a.m.

Now there's just one more change to tomorrow
morning's programme. Lunch will be served in the
Cream Dining-room not the Red one as it says on
the programme.

The programme you have in front of you does not
state which room Professor Aster's lecture will be
in. It'll be at two o'clock as planned and will be in
the Round Hall. There are plenty of signs around
directing you to the Round Hall and the other
rooms we're using.

There are a couple of changes to the seminar
rooms we're using tomorrow afternoon. The
Australian group will be working in room 27 and
the Caribbean group in room 18. 27 and 18 are
rather larger rooms and so lots of you can attend.

One final change. Unfortunately Mark Wright will
not be able to stay for the plenary session on
Sunday morning. He's got to catch a flight early
on Sunday to another conference in Rome. Dr
Anne Cox has kindly agreed to take his place on
the panel.

I hope that that is all clear and that everything will go
smoothly. I should now like to say a bit more about the
facilities in this building....

*(Allow one minute for candidates to complete the
changes.)*

You now have 2 hours 40 minutes to complete the rest
of the paper.

> **Practice Test Two**

PART ONE, PART ONE. *(Allow time to check that
candidates have found PART 1.)*

In this first part you will hear ten sentences. Each
sentence will be said twice. Choose the best reply for
each one. Look at the example. *(15 seconds.)*

If you hear: 'What's the matter? You look very pale', the best answer is C. Put a circle round your answers.

Listen.

Number one, number one. *(5 seconds)*
When do you think we should set off?
When do you think we should set off? *(10 seconds)*

Number two, number two. *(5 seconds)*
She seems to have it in for me.
She seems to have it in for me. *(10 seconds)*

Number three, number three. *(5 seconds)*
It's a bit nippy today, isn't it.
It's a bit nippy today, isn't it. *(10 seconds)*

Number four, number four. *(5 seconds)*
I'm trying to cut out sweet things.
I'm trying to cut out sweet things. *(10 seconds)*

Number five, number five. *(5 seconds)*
Anyone could cope with his job.
Anyone could cope with his job. *(10 seconds)*

Number six, number six. *(5 seconds)*
She's a pain in the neck, isn't she?
She's a pain in the neck, isn't she? *(10 seconds)*

Number seven, number seven. *(5 seconds)*
Are you up to going out tonight?
Are you up to going out tonight? *(10 seconds)*

Number eight, number eight. *(5 seconds)*
John got the sack yesterday.
John got the sack yesterday. *(10 seconds)*

Number nine, number nine. *(5 seconds)*
Don't do anything I wouldn't do.
Don't do anything I wouldn't do. *(10 seconds)*

Number ten, number ten. *(5 seconds)*
No, I insist, it's my treat.
No, I insist, it's my treat. *(10 seconds)*

PART TWO, PART TWO. *(Check that candidates have found PART 2.)*

You are going to add some information to the map of New Zealand. Listen to the instructions and add the information to the map. Study the map first. *(Allow 15 seconds for students to look at the map.)*

I'm now going to read out the instructions which you must follow to complete the map. You will hear the instructions **twice.** Ready?

(Read the instructions at normal reading speed allowing ten seconds between each of them.)

First we are going to name some of the most important towns in New Zealand. Auckland is the most northerly town indicated on the map. Write Auckland, that's A-U-C-K-L-A-N-D, beside the most northerly dot on the map.

Napier is the other town not yet named on the map which is situated on North Island. It is on the south eastern coast. Write Napier, that's N-A-P-I-E-R, beside the appropriate dot.

Dunedin is an attractive little town on the south-east coast of South Island. Write Dunedin, that's D-U-N-E-D-I-N against the dot on the south-east coast of South Island.

Queenstown is inland from Dunedin. Indeed it's the only town of any size in South Island which is not on the coast. Write its name – Q-U-E-E-N-S-T-O-W-N – against its dot on the map.

The only town still to be named on the map is Nelson, which is at the north of South Island opposite Wellington. Write Nelson, N-E-L-S-O-N, beside the dot at the top of South Island.

The water between North and South Island is called Cook Strait. Write Cook Strait, C-O-O-K, S-T-R-A-I-T, between the two islands.

The highest mountain in New Zealand is also called after Cook, the Englishman who explored the South Pacific in the eighteenth century. Mount Cook is halfway up the western coast of South Island. Draw a small triangle to indicate Mount Cook, halfway up the west coast of South Island.

Label the triangle Mount Cook and note its height beside its name. Its height is three thousand seven hundred and sixty-four metres, three thousand seven hundred and sixty-four metres.

On North Island write the name of the lake just south-east of Hamilton and very popular with tourists. It's called Rotorua, that's R-O-T-O-R-U-A.

Finally draw an arrow pointing due west from Auckland and write beside it one thousand three hundred miles. Australia. Australia is one thousand three hundred miles west of Auckland.

(Wait thirty seconds before reading the instructions a second time.)

Now I'll read the instructions again. Ready?

PART THREE, PART THREE. (Check that the candidates have found PART 3.)

You are going to listen to part of a lecture about the American author, John Steinbeck. Listen and complete the notes. You will hear the lecture **once** only. (15 seconds)

Ready? Now listen and complete the notes.

John Steinbeck was born in Salinas in California in 1902 and he died in 1968 at the age of sixty-six. He wrote his first major novel in 1935. It is called *Tortilla Flat* and it depicts life in rural California. Perhaps his most significant novel is *The Grapes of Wrath*. *The Grapes of Wrath* was written in 1939 and it tells of the hardships endured by the poor in America at the time. *The Grapes of Wrath* actually led to political changes to help the poor and thus it was of great social as well as literary importance. It can be compared to the famous nineteenth century novel called *Uncle Tom's Cabin*. *Uncle Tom's Cabin* played a not insignificant role in the abolition of slavery in nineteenth century America. Steinbeck won the Pulitzer Prize for *The Grapes of Wrath*. Other major novels by Steinbeck are *Of Mice and Men* which he wrote in 1937, *The Moon is Down* written in 1942 and *East of Eden* written in 1952. Let me recap, that's *Of Mice and Men*, 1937; *The Moon is Down*, 1942 and *East of Eden*, 1952. In 1962, six years before his death, he received the Nobel Prize for Literature. Several biographies of Steinbeck have been written but I would particularly recommend the one by P. McCarthy. That's M-C, capital C-A-R-T-H-Y. That's P. McCarthy's biography. It was published in 1980 and you should find copies in the library.

You now have 2 hours 40 minutes to complete the rest of the paper.

Practice Test Three

PART ONE, PART ONE. (Allow time to check that candidates have found PART 1.)

In this first part you will hear ten sentences. Each sentence will be said **twice**. Choose the best reply for each one. Look at the example. (15 seconds.)

If you hear: 'What's the matter? You look very pale', the best answer is C. Put a circle round your answers.

Listen.

Number one, number one. (5 seconds)
Have you got a moment?
Have you got a moment? (10 seconds)

Number two, number two. (5 seconds)
I think he must have got out of bed on the wrong side this morning.
I think he must have got out of bed on the wrong side this morning. (10 seconds)

Number three, number three. (5 seconds)
I feel a bit sick.
I feel a bit sick. (10 seconds)

Number four, number four. (5 seconds)
Remember. This is off the record.
Remember. This is off the record. (10 seconds)

Number five, number five. (5 seconds)
I hope we can pull if off.
I hope we can pull it off. (10 seconds)

Number six, number six. (5 seconds)
Whatever gave you that idea?
Whatever gave you that idea? (10 seconds)

Number seven, number seven. (5 seconds)
What's on tonight?
What's on tonight? (10 seconds)

Number eight, number eight. (5 seconds)
What did you make of him?
What did you make of him? (10 seconds)

Number nine, number nine.   *(5 seconds)*
He scraped through the physics exam.
He scraped through the physics exam.   *(10 seconds)*

Number ten, number ten.   *(5 seconds)*
He ticked her off for her behaviour.
He ticked her off for her behaviour.   *(10 seconds)*

PART TWO, PART TWO.   *(Check that candidates
have found PART 2.)*

You have some information about Braille and some
examples of symbols used by Braille but your
information is incomplete. You are going to listen to
someone talking about Braille in order to help you
complete this information. Listen to the speaker and
complete the paragraph. Then follow the instructions
which you will hear.

Study the information and symbols in your book now.
(15 seconds)

You will hear the instructions **twice**.   *(Read the
instructions leaving 10 seconds after each one.)*

First add Braille's nationality and dates to the
information at the top of the page in your book.
Braille was invented by a Frenchman, Louis Braille, in
the first half of the nineteenth century. He was born in
1809 and died in 1852.

His system enables blind people to read and write. It is
a system of embossed dots based on a matrix of two by
three. This allows for a maximum of six dots in any
one symbol. Individual symbols indicate letters,
numbers, punctuation marks and some short words.
Add punctuation marks and some short words to the
notes at the top of your page.

The symbols illustrated in your book all stand for
letters. Beside the symbols write the letters they
represent. The letter A is represented by one dot in the
top left-hand corner. Write A beside the symbol
consisting of a single dot.

The letter R consists of three dots on the left-hand side
and one dot in the centre on the right-hand side. Write
R beside the appropriate symbol.

The letter X consists of two dots on the top line of the
matrix and two on the bottom with an empty central
line. Write X beside the appropriate symbol.

The letter T also consists of four dots. There is one in
the top right-hand corner, there are two on the middle
line and one in the bottom left-hand corner. Write T
beside the appropriate symbol.

The letters E and I both consist of two dots. E has one
dot in the top left-hand corner and one on the right-hand
side of the central line of the matrix. I, on the other
hand, has one dot in the top right-hand corner and one
on the left-hand side of the central line. Write E and I
beside the appropriate symbols.

Now you are going to draw some symbols yourselves.
First draw the symbol for G. G has four dots, two on
the top line and two on the central line.

Now draw the symbol for O. O has a dot in the top left-
hand corner, one on the right-hand side of the central
line and one on the left-hand side of the bottom line.

Now draw the symbol for U. U has three dots. There
are two on the bottom line and one in the top left-hand
corner.

Finally, have a go at J. J has a dot in the top right-hand
corner and two on the central line.

*(Allow candidates 30 seconds and then repeat the
instructions.)*

Now I'll read the instructions again. Ready?

PART THREE, PART THREE.   *(Check that
candidates have found PART 3.)*

Look at the instructions in your book.   *(30 seconds)*
You are going to hear some information about a couple
of different people. You have heard that Patricia may
be interested in sharing a flat with a friend of yours.
Note down everything that you hear about Patricia in
order to tell your friend. You are only interested in the
girl called Patricia. Do not write about anyone else.
You will hear the information **once** only.

I work with a couple of quite interesting people. There's a man called Harry and a girl called Patricia. Curiously enough, Harry and Patricia have got the same surname and quite an unusual one at that, it's Latymer, L-A-T-Y-M-E-R - although they assure me they're not related in any way. They certainly don't look alike. Harry's short and rather fat whereas Patricia's tall and slim. Patricia's hair is dark and straight and she has it even shorter than Harry's, whose is blonde and curly. She's rather an interesting girl, I think. She has some rather unusual hobbies – parachuting and playing the harp. They make quite a contrast, don't they - parachuting and harp-playing? Harry's much more ordinary in his habits – he's into football and motorbikes. He's got a dog at home whereas Patricia keeps a pet snake. I'm not surprised she lives alone. Not many people would be prepared to share a flat with a snake. Patricia's birthday is on American Independence Day, July the fourth. Harry's is two days later on July the sixth. I went to Patricia's last birthday party – she was 22 – and I was surprised to find that she is the youngest of six children. Somehow I'd always imagined she'd be an only child. Like Harry.

Now you have one minute to complete your notes. *(1 minute)*

You now have 2 hours 40 minutes to complete the rest of the paper.

Practice Test Four

PART ONE, PART ONE. *(Allow time to check that candidates have found PART 1.)*

In this first part you will hear ten sentences. Each sentence will be said **twice.** Choose the best reply for each one. Look at the example. *(15 seconds.)*

If you hear: 'What's the matter? You look very pale', the best answer is C. Put a circle round your answers.

Listen.

Number one, number one. *(5 seconds)*
Have you heard the latest?
Have you heard the latest? *(10 seconds)*

Number two, number two. *(5 seconds)*
I hope they make up soon.
I hope they make up soon. *(10 seconds)*

Number three, number three. *(5 seconds)*
Don't forget to take all your belongings with you.
Don't forget to take all your belongings with you. *(10 seconds)*

Number four, number four. *(5 seconds)*
Did you hear the one about the elephant and the zebra crossing?
Did you hear the one about the elephant and the zebra crossing? *(10 seconds)*

Number five, number five. *(5 seconds)*
He's got a terribly big head.
He's got a terribly big head. *(10 seconds)*

Number six, number six. *(5 seconds)*
Shall we hit the road?
Shall we hit the road? *(10 seconds)*

Number seven, number seven. *(5 seconds)*
When should we set our alarms for?
When should we set our alarms for? *(10 seconds)*

Number eight, number eight. *(5 seconds)*
I wish she wouldn't keep bringing that up.
I wish she wouldn't keep bringing that up. *(10 seconds)*

Number nine, number nine. *(5 seconds)*
Surely he can't have guessed the truth.
Surely he can't have guessed the truth. *(10 seconds)*

Number ten, number ten. *(5 seconds)*
You're having me on.
You're having me on. *(10 seconds)*

PART TWO, PART TWO. *(Check that candidates have found PART 2.)*

You are going to correct some mistakes in an article.. Read the article now. *(45 seconds)*

Now listen to a correct version of the story. Circle any information in the article which differs from what you hear. Also write what the article should say beside the circled errors.

You will hear the information **twice**.

(Read the article twice at normal reading speed.)

John Barnet (31) was cycling home along Tennyson Road last night at about 7.00 when a silver Rolls Royce came hurtling round the corner of Somerton Road. Mr Barnet was knocked off his bike but the Rolls Royce did not stop. Fortunately, a colleague of Mr Barnet's, Glenda Smith, was standing at the bus stop in Somerton Way. She heard the crash and John's scream and she ran to the scene just in time to see the car racing round the corner. She believes, however, that the car's registration number was GEI 23. Quick-thinking Ms Smith stopped a passing taxi-cab to radio for an ambulance. This arrived within minutes and Mr Barnet is now recovering in the St Christopher's Hospital, Grant Road. His condition is said to be stable. John's parents were too upset to speak to our reporter but his attractive red-haired cousin, Tina (24), told us 'John is always the most careful of cyclists and has never been involved in an accident in his life.' She added that she had always felt hit and run drivers should be severely fined. Police are appealing for anyone living in the area or anyone who recognises the description of the car to ring the central police station on 433876 and to ask for Sergeant Fred Stanton.

PART THREE, PART THREE. *(Check that candidates have found PART 3.)*

Study the announcements that appeared in the Births column of a local newspaper. You are going to hear some information about a birth. Listen to the information and then write a birth announcement similar to the ones below. You will hear the information **once** only. *(15 seconds)*

(Read the following aloud once only at normal speed.)

I wonder if you'd mind putting this announcement of the birth of our baby girl in the paper for us. It'd be such a help when we're so busy. Try and make sure the newspaper spells our name right as Hadley can be spelt in several different ways. We spell ours H-A-D-L-E-Y, of course. We've decided to call the baby Sarah Jane. I'll spell it for you to avoid confusion,

S-A-R-A-H, J-A-N-E, Sarah Jane. She was actually born on the 16th April. It was only a few minutes after midnight so she just made the 16th, the same day as Ben's birthday. Do mention Ben and Anne in the announcement, just B-E-N and Anne with an E, of course. They usually seem to mention brothers and sisters in birth announcements these days and I think it's nice if they do. That's all, isn't it? No, I should point out that Bob and I would prefer our names to be printed in full, Robin and Alyson – that's Robin, R-O-B-I-N and Alyson, A-L-Y-S-O-N, rather than Bob and Ali. Hope all this is clear. If there are any problems ring us back when you get home. Bye.

You now have five minutes to write the birth announcement. *(5 minutes)*

Stop writing now. You now have 2 hours 40 minutes. to complete the rest of the paper.

Answers to Practice Tests

Practice Test One

Listening

Part 1

1	B	6	C
2	A	7	D
3	B	8	B
4	D	9	D
5	A	10	C

Part 2

Name of cottage	Village	Can sleep	Cost per week	Special notes
Seaview House	Flixton	6	£125	300 years old, 400 metres from beach
Rose Cottage	Flixton	3	£115	Phone – 0231 956
Ivy Retreat	Aldeburgh	4 + baby (cot)	£125	Small swimming pool, tennis court
Journey's End	Aldeburgh	8 (no cot)	£250	Antique furniture, dishwasher etc.

Part 3

Changes to be made:
Friday April 13th
8.00 not 7.30
Inform desk of workshop choice by 8 a.m. on Saturday morning.
Saturday April 4th
Extra morning workshop
C *It's not what you say it's the way that you say it* led by Anne Cox. Seminar Room 35
Lunch in Cream Dining-room not Red one.
Insert Round Hall after Professor Aster's name.
Room changes 22 to 27, 25 to 18
Sunday April 15th
Change Mark Wright to Anne Cox.

English Usage

1	not	11	tells
2	in	12	elsewhere
3	which	13	but
4	to	14	is
5	less	15	despite
6	but	16	trying / attempting
7	for	17	At
8	not	18	Whether
9	to	19	would
10	in	20	worth

Reading One

1 D; 2 D; 3 D; 4 B; 5 B.

Reading Two

Average pocket money	£3.60 per week
Average for 12-year-old	£2.50
Average for 16-year-old	£5.50
Average % increase over last year	4%
Inflation rate	7.7%

QUESTION	% SAYING YES
Do you save regularly?	90%
Do you have a cash-dispenser card? (16-year olds)	76%
Would you consult your parents before making a big decision concerning money?	80%

CRITERION	BEST	WORST
Amount of pocket money received	South-east and London	South-west and western regions
Satisfaction with amount of pocket money received	London and East Anglia	Northern Ireland
Care taken with money received	London	North-west
Possession of a cash-dispenser card	Northern Ireland	
Largest proportion of money spent on clothes	Scotland	Northern Ireland
Largest proportion of money spent on books	Northern Ireland	Scotland
Generosity i.e. tendency to buy presents	South-east	

Reading Three

JOB   Interpreting

Qualities and skills required   discretion; good memory; strong powers of concentration; highly educated; up-to-date with developments in the language; physically and mentally agile; calm under stress

Advantages of job very high salaries; see history in the making

Disadvantages constant security vetting; very stressful; strict discipline; disruptive to home life

Suitability for different sexes, ages etc? 60% are women but n.b. disruptive to home life

Reading and Writing

A suggested answer is provided here to give an idea of the kind of answer expected of the best candidates at this level. In later practice tests, only notes are provided to help with the marking of the reading and writing question.

Dear Maria,

Thanks for your letter. It was good to hear all your news. I'm having a marvellous time here in England and am longing to tell you all about it when I get back.

I've had a great time in bookshops looking at detective novels. There certainly are plenty to choose from. I've picked out six which I think would give you a good variety to write about. Let me know what you think. I'll buy any that you like the sound of and can happily look for others if you'd prefer.

First of all I'd go for something by Dick Francis. My landlady here says he's the best detective story writer she knows. A good example of his work would be *Slay Ride*. It's set around a racecourse in Norway. Apparently, most of his books deal with the racing world in some way.

By way of contrast, why not try one of Ellis Peters' medieval crime stories? One of these is *The Hermit of Eyton Forest*, which takes place in a Benedictine Abbey in 1142. Ellis Peters seems to have written detective stories with a more modern background as well but I thought the historical one could be interesting.

Then how about something by Colin Dexter? His story, *The Silent World of Nicholas Quinn*, is set in the department where they prepare the Oxford exams for foreign students learning English! Maybe the book'll give some insight into how to do well at English exams!

Josephine Tey seems to be another popular writer. One of her books looks a rather different kind of crime story. It's called *The Daughter of Time* and it's based on a true murder mystery in English history, one involving the controversial king, Richard III. I'm certainly going to read that one myself!

There seem to be quite a lot of female detective story writers in English. Another one is Patricia Highsmith. Her book, *The Blunderer*, seems to be about a man murdering his wife – or did he?

My final choice would be Dashiell Hammett's *The Thin Man*. This one is about an American detective who comes out of retirement to solve a violent murder. I thought an American element might give you a bit of extra variety.

Look forward to hearing what you think.
All good wishes,
Felicity

(N.B. It doesn't matter exactly which books are chosen, of course, although the Father Brown stories should be avoided as the writer has already read those. The Simenon story is also not altogether appropriate as it is a translation. It would also make sense not to include two books by the same author.)

Writing

A model composition is provided for one of the compositions here in order to give an impression of the length and complexity of writing expected of the best candidates at this level. In later practice tests no model compositions are provided.

d)

62 Bateman Street
Cambridge
CB2 1LX

The Manager
The Star Hotel
Regent Street
London

5th July 1992

Dear Sir,

Last week I stayed in your hotel from the 25th to the 28th of June. I was extremely disappointed with my stay there. For the prices that you charge I would expect a much better standard of service.

The most serious problem for me was the noise from the disco. I was in London for an important conference at which I needed to be fresh and alert. This was extremely difficult as the disco kept going until three a.m. Because of the heat last week, both the disco and my bedroom had to have their windows open. I know that many of the other residents on that side of the building were as disturbed by the row as I was. Might I suggest that you install air-conditioning into both the disco and the bedrooms so that, even when it is hot, it is not necessary to have windows open?

The food was also disappointing. The menu was uninteresting, the salads were tired and I am sure the soups came out of tins. Worst of all, perhaps, I had to send glasses and cutlery back to the kitchens on three occasions because they had not been properly washed.

Cleanliness was also a problem in the bedrooms. When I arrived I found someone else's hairs in the basin. Not a very promising start to my stay!

When I complained about this at reception, your staff seemed more amused than concerned. I also found the behaviour of your staff rude when I asked for a hot cocoa late at night. I do not think that an unreasonable request in a supposedly quality hotel.

In view of all these problems, might I suggest that you select your staff with greater care in the future? It would also be desirable to keep a much closer eye on how they are performing their duties. I regret to inform you that I must advise my company not to use The Star again.

Yours faithfully,

F. O'Dell (Dr)

Practice Test Two

Listening
Part 1

1	B	6	D
2	C	7	C
3	B	8	B
4	D	9	C
5	C	10	A

Part 2

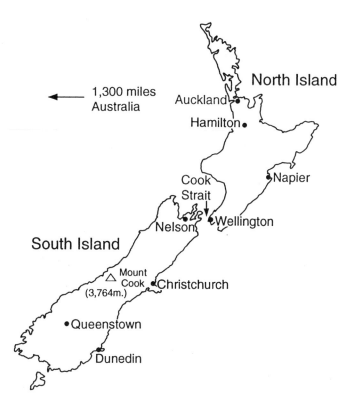

Part 3
Dates: 1902-1968
Background: California
Major Novels with dates:
Tortilla Flat 1935
The Grapes of Wrath 1939
Of Mice and Men 1937
The Moon is Down 1942
East of Eden 1952
Political significance: *The Grapes of Wrath* led to political change to help the poor.
Prizes won: Pulitzer (for *The Grapes of Wrath*) ; Nobel Prize for Literature (1962)
Recommended biography: P.McCarthy (1980)

English Usage

1	for	11	in
2	which	12	to
3	not	13	making
4	as	14	no
5	either	15	but
6	beyond	16	some / most / all
7	what	17	own
8	world	18	with
9	to	19	which
10	will	20	well

Reading One

1 C; 2 C; 3 A; 4 D; 5 B.

Reading Two

Definition of a tourist for the purposes of these statistics – anyone who is away from home overnight.

	Now	30 years ago	In 20 years time
Number of international hotel arrivals	390 million	60 million	780 million

Number of hotel rooms currently available for international tourists	10.5 million
Money spent on international air fares	figures not provided

NATIONALITY	NO. OF TOURISTS
American (US)	44,800,000
British	25,080,000
German	21,250,000
French	9,200,000
Japanese	7,320,000

Reasons for probable increase in tourism over the next
20 years:
1 more people will have passports
2 people will have more holiday entitlement
3 there will be fewer restrictions on the Japanese
4 people from the Far East and newly developing
   countries will start travelling more
5 people from Eastern Europe will travel more

SIZE OF AIRLINER	EXAMPLE	NOS. IN 1989	NOS. IN 2004
under 120 seats	BAC 1-11, DC9, 737-200	2,690	1,292
120-170 seats	Trident 3, 737-400	2,216	3,799
171-240	757, 767, Concorde	955	3,783
240+	747, stretched 767	1,377	3,580

	In hotel business	In tourism generally
Number of people employed	57 million	101 million

Reading Three

1 Head
  Should include:
  a) an attempt to make friends with the audience.
  b) an outline of what you want to say and why.

2 Body
  Advice:
  a) Keep it short and simple.
  b) Select one headline as your main message.
  c) Omit tedious detail.
  d) Give colourful information and use narrative.
  e) Indicate the milestones of your talk, showing where one section ends and another begins. f) Make sections shorter as you progress through talk.

3 Tail
  Advice:
  a) Sum up what talk was about.
  b) Keep it brisk, cheerful and short.
4 Questions and Answers

Reading and Writing

Candidates here should:
give full answers to each of the seven questions
(it would be appropriate simply to write the number of each question and then their answer beside it).

Writing

No model compositions are provided here. For an example of the kind of length and complexity of language expected of the best candidates at Pitman Advanced level, see the model composition provided for the Writing question in Practice Test One.

Practice Test Three

Listening

Part 1

1 B	6 C
2 A	7 A
3 B	8 B
4 A	9 C
5 D	10 D

Part 2

Information to add to paragraph – French, 1809, 1852, punctuation marks and some short words.

The symbols from left to right should be labelled:
–, E, T, R, –, A, –, I, X

The symbols to be drawn are like this.

Part 3

Information to be noted down
Patricia Latymer
tall, slim with dark, straight and very short hair. Hobbies - parachuting, playing the harp. Pet snake. 22, birthday July 4th. Youngest of six children.

English Usage

1	what	11	under
2	to	12	as
3	anyone	13	there
4	from	14	this
5	how	15	order
6	what	16	If/When
7	way	17	cannot
8	is	18	with / in
9	into	19	Third(ly)/Finally
10	on	20	themselves

Reading One

1 C; 2 D; 3 A; 4 D; 5 B.

Reading Two

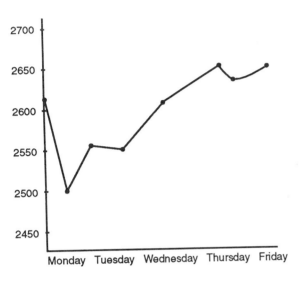

Footsie

Nikkei

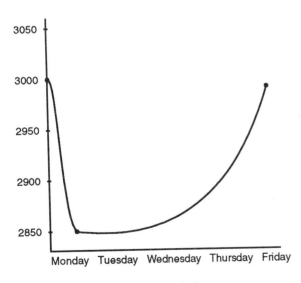

Dow Jones Industrials

Deutsche Aktien

Reading Three

Largest fishing port   Ullapool
Main catch   Mackerel and herring
Catch goes to   a) East Coast markets
  b) Klondykers
Klondykers are East European factory ships
Processed fish is exported to
  a) Eastern Europe
  b) Third World

Attitude of locals to the Klondykers and reason for that attitude Get on well with them because they bring in money to the area at a time when there are few tourists around.
Attitude of Government to the Klondykers and reason for that attitude Want to tax them more as the stocks of fish are declining too fast.
Other fishing ports Mallaig, Kinlochbervie, Lochinver, Oban, Kyle of Lochalsh
Main catch there now Queen scallops and clams
Life for Mallaig's children now Board during the week at school in Fort William.
and in the future Boys may find work on boat but girls, unless they find a job at local fish processing factory, will head for Glasgow.
New fishing industry Fish farming.
Products Lobster, trout, turbot, plaice, shellfish, salmon.
Special characteristics of this way of producing salmon:
  a) simulates in the lochs the life cycle of salmon
  b) fish given their colour by artificial pigment
Advantage of this new industry New jobs created.
Disadvantages   a) Overfeeding of water
  results in excess algae.
  b) Natural resources
  (plankton, micro-organisms,
  etc.) depleted.

Reading and Writing

Candidates here should:
cover all four areas indicated by asterisks in the announcement
give concrete examples
write in a way that would be interesting and informative for readers of an international magazine

Writing

No model compositions are provided here. For an example of the kind of length and complexity of language expected of the best candidates at Pitman Advanced level, see the model composition provided for the Writing question in Practice Test One.

Practice Test Four

Listening
Part 1

1	A	6	D
2	C	7	C
3	B	8	B
4	D	9	C
5	B	10	C

Part 2
Changes:
21 to 31
7.30 to 7.00
red Rolls to silver
Way to Road
Smayle to Smith
JAI to GEI
girlfriend to cousin
20 to 24
438876 to 433876
Frank to Fred

Part 3
HADLEY: To Robin and Alyson a daughter, Sarah Jane, born 16th April, a sister for Ben and Anne.

English Usage

1	with	11	any/elsewhere
2	on	12	at
3	in	13	where
4	other	14	able
5	If	15	under
6	else	16	considering
7	there	17	unless / until
8	most	18	Why
9	all	19	on/into
10	on	20	being

Reading One

1 B; 2 D; 3 C; 4 C; 5 A.

Reading Two

Top row
From left to right – 11 H; 1 F; 16 E; 8 I; 5 D.
Bottom row
From left to right – 7 C; 2 A; 14 J; 9 B; 6 G.

Reading Three

TYPE OF COMPANY	TO SET UP YOU MUST:	ADVANTAGES	DISADVANTAGES
Sole trader	No legal formalities but must keep books for tax purposes.	Freedom and independence. You get all profits.	Unlimited personal responsibility for any losses.
Partnership	No legal formalities required although a partnership deed is advisable.	Share responsibility.	Each partner personally responsible to outside creditors even if partner caused the debt. May remain responsible even when retired from partnership.
Company	Submit various documents to Registrar of Companies. Pay fee.	Have limited personal liability for debts incurred.	Cost at start-up and on doing annual paperwork. Lose privacy.

Reading and Writing

Candidates here should:
begin with a general statement of what the graph shows
describe the main trends provided by the graph
make some comments on points that interest or surprise

Writing

No model compositions are provided here. For an example of the kind of length and complexity of language expected of the best candidates at Pitman Advanced level, see the model composition provided for the Writing question in Practice Test One.